HEALTH CARE POLICY IN THE UNITED STATES

edited by

JOHN G. BRUHN
PENNSYLVANIA STATE
UNIVERSITY-HARRISBURG

A GARLAND SERIES

Health Care Policy in the United States
John G. Bruhn, editor

HELPING SURVIVORS OF DOMESTIC VIOLENCE

THE EFFECTIVENESS OF MEDICAL, MENTAL HEALTH, AND COMMUNITY SERVICES

JUDITH S. GORDON

GARLAND PUBLISHING, INC.
A MEMBER OF THE TAYLOR & FRANCIS GROUP
NEW YORK & LONDON / 1998

RAP 4648494

Library of Congress Cataloging-in-Publication Data

Gordon, Judith S., 1958–
    Helping survivors of domestic violence : the effectiveness of
medical, mental health, and community services / Judith S. Gordon.
        p.   cm. — (Health care policy in the United States)
    Includes bibliographical references and index.
    ISBN 0-8153-3330-7 (alk. paper)
    1. Abused women—United States—Psychology. 2. Abused
women—United States—Health aspects. 3. Abused women—
United States—Family relationships. 4. Abused women—Counseling of—United States. 5. Victims of family violence—United
States. 6. Women—Abuse of—United States. 7. Battered woman
syndrome—United States. I. Title. II. Series: Health care policy
in the United States (New York, N.Y.)
HV6626.2.G67 1998
362.82'92—dc21
                                                                98-39288

Printed on acid-free, 250-year-life paper
Manufactured in the United States of America

For Paul, Rachel, and Sarah.

Contents

v

Contents

Figures

Tables

Acknowledgments

I wish to express my sincere appreciation to Drs. Anne Simons, Robert Weiss, Robert Mauro, and Larry Irvin for their important contributions throughout every phase of this project. I also wish to thank my mentors and colleagues at the Oregon Research Institute, especially Dr. Judy Andrews, Pamela Unfried, Barbara Eisenhardt, and Laura Akers, for their invaluable help in the planning, data collection, analysis, and writing stages of this work.

In addition, I am indebted to the staff and volunteers of Womenspace in Eugene, Oregon, for allowing me to conduct my study, and to the women who use their services, whose voices are heard throughout this book.

Finally, I wish to give my most heart-felt thanks to my husband, Paul Schwyhart, for his sense of humor and unfailing support and encouragement of my endeavors, without which I could not have accomplished my goals.

This investigation was supported in part by a grant from the Oregon Research Institute, Eugene, Oregon.

Helping Survivors of Domestic Violence

CHAPTER I

What Is Domestic Violence?

SCOPE OF THE PROBLEM

The problem of domestic violence is widespread in the United States. While abuse to men by women, and mutual violence, occurs within abusive relationships, the majority of domestic violence cases involve men's abusive behavior towards women, and that abuse has the most serious consequences (Cantos, Neidig, & O'Leary, 1991; Vivian & Langhinrichsen-Rohling, 1994; Walker, 1979). According to a recent Surgeon General's report (USDHHS, 1991), assault by an intimate is the leading cause of injury among women, greater than automobile accidents, muggings, and cancer deaths combined. Current estimates suggest that two to three million women are assaulted by male partners each year in the United States (Straus & Gelles, 1990) and that 21–34% of all women will be assaulted by a male partner at some point in their lives. Straus and Gelles (1990) report a 1985 survey which showed that in almost one eighth of married couples, the husband had carried out one or more acts of physical aggression against their wives during the previous 12 months. The same study showed that at least 1.8 million husbands severely assaulted their wives to the point of hospitalization, making domestic violence the number one cause of emergency room admissions for women in the United States.

Data collected by the Judiciary Committee to the United States Senate (Violence Against Women, 1992), showed that during 1991, 21,000 domestic crimes against women were reported to the police every week and almost 20% of aggravated assaults reported to the police took place in the home. These figures reveal a total of at least 1.1 million assaults, aggravated assaults, murders, and rapes against women committed in the home and reported to the police in 1991 alone. The United States Senate (Violence Against Women, 1992) suggests that unreported crimes may be more than three times this total. Applying these statistics to Lane County, approximately 13,000 women will experience at least one violent episode in their homes this year; over 6,500 of these women will receive severe and repeating beatings.

TYPES OF ABUSE

Abuse in relationships may include physical violence such as pushing, shoving, slapping, punching, and shooting, and sexual coercion and assault (e.g., use of objects, uncomfortable/embarrassing sexual experiences, rape, etc.) (Goodman et al., 1993; Straus, 1990). In addition to these crimes of physical violence, another powerful form of control used by many abusers is psychological or verbal abuse. These "psychological attacks" may consist of intimidation, intense criticisms, insults, threats of bodily harm (to the victim, children, or abuser) and brainwashing (Pagelow, 1981; Walker, 1979). Another form of control commonly used is social abuse, which consists of isolation, restraint from activities, denial of resources, and reinforcement of traditional female roles (Pagelow, 1981; Walker, 1979).

Anecdotal evidence from counselors and abused women suggests that in the long term, non-physical abuse may be even more damaging than physical violence (Information gathered as Facilitator of Womenspace Community Support Group, 1991-1994). While psychological abuse is acknowledged to have major impacts on women (Herman, 1992; Pagelow, 1992; Walker, 1984), most of the research on domestic violence has centered on the causes and consequences of physical and sexual abuse. This is due, in most part, to the difficulty in measuring non-physical forms of abuse (Bowker, 1988; Gelles & Straus, 1990; Straus & Gelles, 1990).

While the literature provides ample statistical information on physical and sexual violence, there are currently no estimates of the prevalence and reporting rates of psychological and social abuse. However, in their study of 234 women with a history of physical abuse, Follingstad and her colleagues (1991) found that 98% had reported emotional abuse as well. In addition, Ewing (1987), in his study of 420 battered women, reported that approximately 50% of the subjects were socially and physically isolated. Walker (1984) found that 34% of the

435 abused women she surveyed had no access to checking accounts, 51% had no access to charge accounts, and 27% had no access to cash.

CONSEQUENCES OF DOMESTIC VIOLENCE

Each year approximately one million women seek medical assistance for injuries related to physical abuse by an intimate (Stark & Flitcraft, 1988). The consequences of violence towards women by their partners range from chronic headaches, sleeping and eating disorders, and multiple injuries to the head, neck, abdomen, and vaginal area (Randall, 1990; Russell, 1982) to death. Between one third and half of all murders of women are committed by their male partners (Carmody & Williams, 1987; Rose & Goss, 1989).

Survivors of domestic violence experience a wide range of psychological problems. The long term impact of abuse includes depression, fear, anxiety, lowered self-esteem, and Posttraumatic Stress Disorder (PTSD) (Browne, 1992; Gelles & Straus, 1988; Walker, 1984). Specific depressive symptoms include blunted affect, numbed responsiveness (Douglas, 1986), reduced social involvement (Hilberman, 1980), feelings of worthlessness (Gelles & Straus, 1988; Mitchell & Hodson, 1983), and increased levels of suicidal ideation and successful suicide (Hilberman, 1980; Stark & Flitcraft, 1988). Victims of abuse experience high levels of anxiety (Stark, Flitcraft, & Frazier, 1979; Walker, 1984). Symptoms of anxiety include sleeping and concentration difficulties (Douglas, 1986) and agitation and hypervigilance (Hilberman, 1980). High rates of PTSD have also been reported among battered women (Kemp, Green, Hovantiz, & Rawlings, 1995; Saunders, 1994; Walker, 1991). The PTSD symptoms experienced by abused women include intrusive memories, nightmares, and avoidance of situations and reminders of the abuse (Saunders, 1994). Several studies have documented lower levels of self-esteem in victims of domestic violence (Mitchell & Hodson, 1983; Trimpey, 1989; Walker, 1979).

CHARACTERISTICS OF BATTERED WOMEN

Women of all class levels, educational backgrounds, and racial and ethnic groups are battered. A study conducted at Midwestern State University (Moewe, 1992) found that more than 50% of women who reported being abused by their spouse had a family income above

$35,000. According to Schulman (1979), 11% of lower income women reported some incident of spousal violence in 1978, compared to 10% of women with family incomes of between $15,000 and $24,000, and 8% of women with family incomes of $25,000 or above. Cazenave and Straus (1990), citing the National Family Survey (NFS), found that the level of violence was greatest in households with an income of between $6,000 and $11,999, while all other income categories ($0–$5,999, $12,000–$19,999, and $20,000+) showed approximately equal (and much lower) levels of abuse.

Findings are mixed regarding racial differences in domestic violence. Cazenave and Straus (1990) report that the rates of spousal violence were greater for African-Americans than for Caucasians. However, when income and occupational level of the abuser were controlled for, this difference between races disappeared. Schulman (1979) found that just over 70% of the victims in his study were Caucasian, 10.4% were African-American, and 9.5% were Hispanic. This same study showed that 33.5% of the abused women held professional occupations, 22% worked in clerical jobs, and 16.7% reported working in the home. Stets and Straus (1990) report different demographics from the NFS. They found that approximately 30% of abused women in their sample held "blue collar" jobs, while 27% had "white collar" occupations; the remainder of the sample either worked in the home or did not report employment status.

Over eighty-seven per cent of the respondents to the Midwestern State University survey had attended college, 33% had earned a college degree, and 18.9% had received a high school diploma or equivalent (Oppel, 1992). Schulman (1979) found that 14.5% of women reporting an incident of abuse had at least attended college, 65.9% had received a high school diploma, and 19.6% had completed eighth grade.

Results from the National Family Survey (Gelles and Cornell, 1990) indicate that all forms of marital violence occur most frequently among those under 30 years of age, at a rate more than double that for the next older age group (31 to 50). This survey also showed a mean age of 30 for abused women who seek help from agencies or shelters. Schulman (1979) indicates that 12% of women aged 18-29 report some incident of violence, compared to 9% of women aged 30-49 and 3% for women aged 50 and over.

COMMUNITY AND PROFESSIONAL SERVICES FOR ABUSED WOMEN

A variety of community services and formal help-sources are available to abused women. The most commonly consulted formal help-sources are the police, social service agencies, crisis counselors, physicians, psychologists, counselors, lawyers, women's groups and the clergy (Bowker, 1988; Bowker & Maurer, 1986; Donato & Bowker, 1984; Frieze, et al., 1980; Hamilton & Coates, 1993; Pagelow, 1981; Tutty, et al., 1993). These services include both professional services (e.g., police, lawyers, physicians, counselors, etc.) and a variety of social support organizations, such as support groups and the clergy. Previous studies suggest that the criminal justice system is the most widely used service , followed by social service agencies, medical services, crisis counseling, psychological services, clergy, support groups, and women's shelters (Bowker, 1988; Bowker & Maurer, 1986; Donato & Bowker, 1984; Frieze, et al., 1980; Hamilton & Coates, 1993; Pagelow, 1981; Tutty, et al., 1993). While many women seek help from professional and/or social service agencies, it should be noted that almost half of all women who report being abused never seek formal assistance (Straus, 1990; Walker, 1979).

The Criminal Justice System

The criminal justice system, consisting of police, lawyers, and judges, is used more often by abused women than any other service (Bowker, 1984; Schulman, 1979; Strube, 1988). There is wide variation in the estimates of women reporting abuse. According to the National Family Violence Survey (Kantor & Straus, 1980), the number of domestic assault victims (mostly women) are approximately 1.8 million per year. Straus & Gelles (1990) report that of women experiencing physical assault, only 6–10% will report the abuse to the police. However, according to Gamache, et al. (1988), between one-third and one-half of battered women had called the police at some time during their lives to report abuse. The disparate estimates are due primarily to the methodological differences between the studies.

According to Bowker (1984), 53% of battered women contacted the police at least once. As violence continues, battered women turn increasingly to formal help sources. Women who were hit frequently (weekly to daily) were most likely to call the police to intervene

(Strube, 1988). In a study of 270 abused women, Hamilton and Coates (1993) found that women suffering physical abuse were most likely to contact police, whereas women experiencing other types of abuse were more likely to consult other services. Women who were victims of emotional and/or sexual abuse were less likely to turn to the police for assistance. In addition, Gelles (1987) found that women working outside the home were more likely to contact the police or other social service agencies than women who work within the home.

Sirles and her colleagues (1993) report that police may use a wide range of tactics when dealing with domestic violence, from informal mediation to arrest. Women victims of abuse may be referred to a social service agency, or to a shelter or women's group in order to receive services within a safe environment.

Social Service Agencies, Physicians and Mental Health Professionals

Social service agencies (social workers, child protective agencies, welfare, etc.) are almost as widely used as, and are often used in conjunction with, the criminal justice system (Bowker, 1984; Schulman, 1979; Strube, 1988). Due to the physical injuries sustained by many abused women, physicians and nurses in hospitals (especially emergency room staff) and in private practice are often contacted (Bowker, 1984; Schulman, 1979; Strube, 1988). Battered women are also likely to visit mental health professionals, such as psychiatrists, psychologists and counselors.

Frieze and her colleagues (1980), in an early study of abused women that used a control group, report that 43% of the sample contacted social service agencies and that 42% sought help from a psychologist or counselor. Pagelow (1981) states that over 40% of her sample of 350 abused women used the services of a psychologist or marriage counselor.

Bowker and Maurer (1986), and Donato and Bowker (1984) report the results of a study that included questionnaire and interview responses by 1,000 abused women. The results of this study indicate that abused women were much more likely to receive help from social service agencies and counselors than from the clergy or women's groups. Over half of their sample received services from social services agencies or counselors, while only one-third consulted the clergy, and one-fifth participated in women's groups. This phenomenon might be attributed to the greater availability of social service agencies and counselors over women's groups in most parts of the country (Bowker & Maurer, 1986), or may be related to the socioeconomic status of the women seeking help (Pagelow, 1981). Women with fewer resources (economic and personal) may be more likely to seek help from service organizations in order to take care of daily survival needs (e.g., housing, food, etc.) and may be less likely to have time to attend a support group.

The Hamilton and Coates (1993) study indicates that victims of psychological abuse were more likely to contact social workers, clergy, and physicians, while victims of sexual abuse more often used the services of psychologists, social workers, psychiatrists, and police. This interesting finding may be due, in part, to societal norms that are beginning to condemn the use of physical and sexual violence against women, but still tacitly approve of emotional coercion and assault. When women are physically and/or sexually assaulted, they have institutional recourse against their abusers through the legal justice system and feel justified in the use of specialized services (e.g., psychologists, etc.). Women who are verbally attacked may be unsure if they are experiencing "abuse" as defined by social institutions. These women may use more general resources, such as family doctors or case workers, to deal with their problems.

Social service agencies provide a wide range of services to abused women. Social workers and welfare case managers assist displaced homemakers with obtaining monetary support and making decisions regarding housing, education, health care and other daily survival needs. Child protection services help battered women and their children to cope with the effects of abuse by offering residential treatment programs for children and community education programs for parents. Since domestic violence is the leading cause of injury among women in this country, physicians and nurses are often called upon (especially in emergency room settings) to treat battered women for the effects of physical and sexual abuse. Private practice physicians, psychologists, and counselors provide a variety of mental health services to assist both women and their children to deal with the results of all forms of abuse.

The Clergy

Members of the clergy are a frequently contacted informal source of help. Many abused women confide in their religious leaders because the clergy are familiar and they feel that the clergy will keep their secrets in confidence (Bowker, 1988; Bowker & Maurer, 1986; Horton et al., 1988). Bowker and Maurer (1986; 1988) found that 33% of the women in their study had contacted the clergy regarding domestic violence. In the Horton et al. study, 48% of abused women turned to their religious leader for help. Religious women may be more likely to turn to their pastor, minister or priest than to "outsiders," such as the police or mental health professionals when discussing abuse (Horton, 1988).

Many churches and religious leaders offer both financial and practical support to victims of domestic violence. Churches will often provide monetary support and/or goods to women who are displaced from their homes due to abuse. In addition, most clergy members provide free counseling services to individuals and couples, and some churches offer subsidized professional counseling. A few churches also sponsor programs to educate their congregations about domestic violence.

Crisis Counseling

Crisis counseling consists of telephone (primarily) or personal contact between abused women and staff (both paid and volunteer) trained by local battered women's shelters or domestic violence coalitions (Murty and Roebuck; 1992). It appears that crisis hot-lines provide a much needed service to abused women. The easy access and anonymity of a telephone-based service are crucial factors in understanding the utilization of hot-lines by abused women.

Several studies indicate that abused women often turn to crisis counselors (Bowker & Maurer, 1986; Donato & Bowker, 1984; Frieze, et al., 1980; Hamilton & Coates, 1993; Murty & Roebuck, 1992; Pagelow, 1981). Murty and Roebuck (1992) analyzed over 4,500 calls to an Atlanta battered women's crisis hot-line. The study reports that the Atlanta Council for Battered Women received an average of 185 crisis calls per month during the two-year study period. Of these calls, 65% were from first-time callers, 20% were from repeat callers, and

15% of the calls were made by third-party callers (other than the victim or abuser), mostly family and friends of the victim.

Crisis counselors provide support to abused women, information and education on domestic violence, and referrals to other help-sources, such as lawyers, psychologists, and support groups. The primary service provided during crisis calls was direct counseling regarding the abusive situation (74%). According to Murty and Roebuck (1992), the counselors who received the crisis calls advised most of the women (85%) to seek further counseling beyond the telephone counseling services (e.g., individual therapy, group participation, shelter residency, etc.).

Shelters

The shelter movement in the United States paralleled the women's movement of the 1970s (Walker, 1979). The first shelters were merely rooms, or couches, in the homes of survivors of domestic violence. These women opened their houses and provided support for other women seeking an end to their abuse. Over the past two decades, battered women's shelters have evolved into multi-faceted service organizations. Shelters for abused women provide a safe haven as well as counseling, advocacy, educational programs and information about various alternatives to living with violence (Pagelow, 1981; Sedlak, 1988). In addition, battered women's shelters are generally the center for a variety of community services, such as crisis lines, outreach programs and support groups.

Horton et al., (1988) found that 38% of their sample of 187 abused women had contacted and/or used the services of a battered women's shelter. Pagelow's (1981) seminal study of domestic violence included information gathered from questionnaires and unstructured interviews from 350 abused women, all of whom had used the services provided by a shelter. Not only do abused women call upon shelters for assistance, but their families and friends, local service agencies, police, physicians, and lawyers all benefit from the information and recommendations provided by shelter staff (Murty & Roebuck, 1992). Murty and Roebuck (1992) report that 15% of the calls received at the Atlanta Council for Battered Women were from third-party callers.

Support Groups

One of the least studied services provided by domestic violence shelters/agencies is the community support group. Support groups are essentially self-help groups, although they are usually led by someone with counseling training. Often the facilitator (or co-facilitator, since most of these groups use more than one leader to avoid the traditional power structure of a therapy group) is a survivor of domestic violence (Donato & Bowker, 1984; Tutty, et al., 1993). Support groups are considered the treatment of choice for abused women by many practitioners (Bowker & Maurer, 1986; Donato & Bowker, 1984; Pagelow, 1981; Tutty, et al., 1993; Walker, 1979), primarily because of the encouraging, empowering nature of this type of group work. Within the safe, non-controlling environment of a support group, abused women can end their isolation and explore options for a violence-free existence.

Several studies (Bowker & Maurer, 1986; Donato & Bowker, 1984; Hamilton & Coates, 1993; Tutty, et al., 1993) indicate that women's groups are not one of the most commonly contacted resources, despite the fact that they provided some of the most specialized services for abused women. This lack of utilization may be due to the limited availability of these groups in many areas (Bowker, 1988; Bowker & Maurer, 1986; Donato & Bowker, 1984) or may be a result of the stigma abused women feel about revealing their abuse, especially in small communities (Pagelow, 1981, Walker, 1979). Attending a support group may be extremely problematic for a women whose abuser is a prominent member of the community. She may feel embarrassed and ashamed because neither she nor her abuser can remain anonymous once she attends a group open to the public.

Support groups offer women the opportunity to share their experiences of living with domestic violence. In addition, group facilitators provide education and information about domestic violence as well as referrals to other community resources (e.g., legal services, counselors, and children's services). Group members are also encouraged to cultivate and maintain their connections outside of the group in order to form an active support system. Most support groups are open to new members each week (i. e., "drop-in" group membership) and are time unlimited. However some groups (e. g., those for specialized populations) offered by women's shelter staff or counselors require registration and are time limited.

CHAPTER II
Review of the Literature

Review of the Literature

DOMESTIC VIOLENCE RESEARCH

Domestic violence research has proliferated since the advent of the women's movement in Great Britain and the United States in the 1970s. Much of this research has focused on the frequency, demography, and interpersonal process variables related to intimate abuse (Blackman, 1989; Breiner, 1992; Fagan & Browne, 1994; Frieze & Browne, 1989; Lie & Gentlewarrier, 1991; O'Leary et al., 1994; Rosenbaum & O'Leary, 1981; Stahly, 1978), including assessment of the characteristics of both batterers and survivors of abuse. This research was designed to describe the phenomenon of partner abuse and to aid researchers and clinicians in dealing with the problem of domestic violence.

Other studies attempt to determine the characteristics of abused women who seek help with their abusive relationships (Cazenave and Straus, 1990; Follingstad, et al., 1991; Gelles & Straus, 1989; Kantor & Straus, 1990; Margolin, 1988; Moewe, 1992; Murty & Roebuck, 1992; Schulman, 1979). These studies have focused on socioeconomic variables (e.g., SES), abuse history (e.g., witnessing or experiencing abuse as a child), attitudes (e.g., traditional gender role beliefs), physical characteristics (e.g., head injury, cognitive difficulties), and psychological characteristics(e.g., psychopathology, depression, anxiety, self-esteem) as predictors of who will become victims of domestic abuse. These studies have been inconclusive and/or contradictory, and no consistent predictors of victimization have been found (Cascardi, O'Leary, Lawrence, & Schlee, 1995; Hotaling &

Sugarman, 1990; Lewis, 1987). Hotaling and Sugarman (1986) concluded that "there is no evidence that the status a woman occupies, the role she performs, the behavior she engages in, her demographic profile or her personality characteristics consistently influence her chance of intimate victimization" (p. 118), and that "men's violence is men's behavior. As such, it is not surprising that the more fruitful efforts to explain this behavior have focused on male characteristics" (p. 120).

In contrast to research on victims of domestic abuse, many studies have isolated batterer characteristics that predict who will engage in different types of domestic abuse. (Hamberger & Hastings, 1991; Holtzworth-Munroe & Stuart, 1994; Hurlbert et al., 1991; Margolin & Burman, 1993; Murphy et al., 1993; Tolman & Bennett, 1990). These studies focus on both individual (e.g., personality characteristics and family history of abuse) and societal (e.g., legal ramifications of domestic violence) factors that contribute to intimate violence.

Research has found that perpetrators of domestic violence vary along a number of important dimensions, including severity of violence, anger, depression, attitudes toward women, psychopathology and/or personality disorders, and alcohol abuse (Faulk, 1974; Gondolf & Fisher, 1988; Hamberger & Hastings, 1991; Hershorn & Rosenbaum, 1991; Shields, McCall, & Hanneke, 1988). Three major dimensions have been found to distinguish among subtypes of batterers: severity of domestic abuse, generality of violence (e.g., family only, or other criminal violence), and psychopathology. In a review of batterer typologies, Holtzworth-Munroe and Stuart (1994) proposed that "family-only" batterers who engage in less severe abuse, make up approximately 50% of perpetrators; "dysphoric/borderline" batterers, account for about 25% of batterers, and commit moderate to severe domestic abuse that is generally confined to family members; and, the last 25% is made up of "generally violent/antisocial" batterers who engage in moderate to severe violence that is not confined to the family.

Several researchers have postulated that batterer typology would be predictive of treatment outcome for perpetrators of domestic abuse (Cadsky & Crawford, 1988; Gondolf & Fisher, 1988). For example, Cadsky & Crawford (1988) hypothesized that "generally violent/antisocial" batterers are unlikely to benefit from the standard cognitive behavioral treatment available for perpetrators of domestic abuse. However, to date, no empirical studies have examined the relation between batterer typologies and the efficacy of treatment for domestic violence.

STUDIES ON PERCEIVED EFFECTIVENESS OF SUPPORT SERVICES

Several studies have attempted to determine the effectiveness of specific community services or interventions based on particular, objective criteria, such as decreased cost of medical treatment for battered women and reduction of domestic violence (Dobash & Dobash, 1987; Gamache, et al., 1988; Gelles & Straus, 1990; McEvoy, et al., 1983). Fewer still seek information on the helpfulness and effectiveness of these help sources from those who use them—abused women.

Abused women seek refuge for the violent acts committed against them by contacting community and professional services. However, few studies have focused on abused women and their help-seeking experiences, or even included the reactions of these women to their experiences. The few early studies in this area (Frieze et al., 1980; Pagelow, 1981; Schulman, 1979) reveal a less than helpful response from many social service agencies and professionals. As stated above, the studies reviewed show that police, social service agencies, clergy, crisis lines, physicians, psychotherapists, women's groups, and lawyers were the most frequently contacted sources of assistance. However, these studies reveal that the most frequently contacted services were not necessarily perceived as the most useful or effective.

Overall, it appears that women find crisis counselors, psychologists and/or counselors, physicians, social workers and lawyers to be helpful when dealing with most types of abuse. However, many women did not find any outside resource to be helpful, and relied mainly on family members and friends for assistance. Most studies on perceived effectiveness report that women find different types of community resources helpful depending on the type of abuse suffered. A discussion of each type of service and it's perceived helpfulness follows.

The Criminal Justice System

The police received significantly lower ratings than did other help sources (Frieze et al., 1980; Hamilton & Coates, 1993; Pagelow, 1981;

Schulman, 1979). Frieze and her colleagues report that abused women found that contacting the police was as likely to intensify the abuse as to curtail it. A study by Pagelow (1981) concurred with the heavy criticism of police for their inadequate response to the women. This study also noted that abused women found that lawyers were more helpful than psychologists, psychiatrists, and the clergy in ending the abuse.

In a unique study of 270 abused women, Hamilton and Coates (1993) examined not only abused women's ratings of help-sources, but also asked participants to identify helpful and non-helpful responses made by the community and professional service workers. They distributed questionnaires among 124 professional offices and service agencies in a small urban area (population of 60,000). Participants in this study reported that police officers were among the most frequently contacted but least helpful groups. Unhelpful responses by the police included "questioned my story," "criticized me for staying in the relationship," and "not informing me of other agencies or professional services." The results of this study are difficult to interpret, however, because the authors never define what they (or the participants) mean by "helpful" or "non-helpful," and a copy of the questionnaire is not included.

Bowker and his colleagues (1984, 1986, 1988) conducted a study of 1,000 abused women; 854 completed questionnaires only, and 146 were interviewed in addition to filling out a questionnaire. The results of this study indicated that 39% of the women found the police to be somewhat to very effective in reducing or ending the abuse. However, 19% of the participants reported that contacting the police caused increased violence. These studies indicate that police response to abused women is not perceived as effective, and may even be detrimental, even though police officers in many areas receive special training in dealing with domestic violence.

New laws concerning domestic violence response by the police and judicial system may be beginning to have a minor impact on the reduction and prevention of abuse (Sirles et al., 1993). In a study of 20 abused women whose abusers were arrested and entered into a violence treatment program according to mandatory arrest and sentencing laws, Sirles and her colleagues (1993) indicate that despite numerous comments expressing dissatisfaction with the legal system, 85% of the women would report violence if it occurred again.

Social Service Agencies, Physicians and Mental Health Professionals

The reviewed studies included wide variations in perceived effectiveness of social services, physicians, psychologists, counselors, and crisis counselors. For example, Frieze and her colleagues (1980) report that abused women rated social service agencies, therapists, and priests approximately equal in helpfulness in ending their victimization, while Pagelow (1981) found that their participants rated lawyers and marriage counselors more helpful than psychologists, psychiatrists, and the clergy.

In their study, Bowker (1988), Bowker and Maurer (1986), and Donato and Bowker (1984) found that the four most effective help sources for eliminating physical and sexual violence, based on direct effectiveness ratings, were women's groups, battered women's shelters, lawyers, and social service/ counseling agencies. Of the 1,000 women who returned surveys, 146 were interviewed in depth. Based on personal experience, these women rated social service/counseling agencies as an effective means for eliminating their partners' violent behavior. Upon further interview, these women cited assistance by the agencies in their effort to separate or divorce from their abusers as most helpful.

As stated earlier, Hamilton and Coates (1993) discovered that, with the exception of social workers and crisis counselors, abused women used different resources depending on the type of abuse encountered. The participants in their study reported that personal crisis counselors, social workers, psychologists, psychiatrists, and physicians were helpful most of the time for all types of abuse. Crisis counselors and social workers were rated as helpful most often for emotional and physical abuse, and were also highly rated for their helpfulness with sexual abuse. The professions most frequently reported as helpful in situations of sexual abuse were psychologists, psychiatrists, physicians, crisis counselors, and social workers.

The participants in Hamilton and Coates (1993) study identified "listening respectfully" and "believing my story" as the two most helpful responses for women experiencing all types of abuse. These responses might be described as the basic skills necessary for the development of good rapport between "therapist" and "client." By hearing abused women and empathizing with their plight, those in the helping professions provide a safe atmosphere in which these women can examine their abusive relationships. The participants reported that responses of "helping me see my strengths" and "helping me see how I'd been losing self-confidence" were most helpful in dealing with emotional abuse. Regarding physical abuse, the responses of "asking if I was being physically hurt" and "helping me see the danger to my children and myself" were ranked most highly. "Letting me know that I am not alone" and "recognizing the impact the abuse had on me" were viewed as most helpful in response to sexual abuse. These responses may be perceived as helpful because they address the issue of self-esteem (which is greatly reduced in abused women), confront the real danger of being in an abusive relationship (rather than pathologizing the women), and assist in removing women from their isolation.

The Clergy

Abused women who are affiliated with a religion may turn first to members of the clergy for help. Women often turn to their religious leaders because the women feel comfortable with someone familiar that they can trust to maintain their secrets in confidence (Bowker & Maurer, 1986; Horton et al., 1988). While the familiarity of the clergy is comforting to many abused women, this intimacy may work against battered women since the clergy may be familiar with (and possibly sympathetic to) their abusers as well (Pagelow, 1981). In addition, members of the clergy are often committed to maintaining the marriage and may suggest that the women return to their abusers (Walker, 1979). While the use of the clergy may be beneficial to some abused women, for others it may reinforce their abusive relationships.

According to several studies (Bowker & Maurer, 1986; Frieze et al., 1980; Pagelow, 1981), although some abused women report being helped by the clergy, most rate the type of counseling provided as unhelpful. Horton and her colleagues report that 54% of the "religious" participants in their study contacted their religious leaders, while 38% of the "nonreligious" participants sought help from the clergy. Of the "religious" women, only 14% found the clergy to be helpful in ending the abuse, and only 3% of the "nonreligious" women reported religious leaders to be helpful. Those women who reported positive experiences with the clergy described the responses they received as "validating" and "supportive." The most positive responses were to religious leaders who agreed that safety, even if it meant divorce, was imperative for the abused women. The most negative responses were to clerics who recommended staying in the relationship and advocated that the women change in order to please their abusers.

Support Groups and Battered Women's Shelters

While not the most frequently used service, women's support groups and shelters are often rated as the most helpful and effective means of coping with abuse (Bowker, 1988; Bowker & Maurer, 1986; Donato & Bowker, 1984; Horton et al., 1988; Pagelow, 1981; Trimpey, 1989; Tutty, et al., 1993). In the Bowker et al. studies (1984, 1986, 1988), 60% of abused women rated staying at shelters or participating in women's groups as very successful in ending the abuse (at least temporarily). The women interviewed reported that the groups (a service provided by shelters) were helpful in raising self-esteem and enabling the women to become more independent. The support groups provided more sessions and a longer period of service to abused women than any of the other resources.

Horton and her colleagues (1988) conducted a study of 187 formerly abused women who had been out of abusive relationships for at least one year. Forty percent of the participants in their study reported that shelters, women's groups, crisis lines, and counseling were helpful in ending the abuse.

In a study of 36 members of a battered women's support group, Trimpey (1989) reports that the participants suffered from low self-esteem and higher-than-average levels of global anxiety. After participation in the group program, self-esteem and coping skills significantly increased, while levels of anxiety decreased, although they were still higher than "normal."

Tutty and her colleagues (1993) evaluated the effectiveness of twelve community-based battered women's support groups. The researchers found that participation in a support group was associated with significant positive change on a number of outcome measures, including self-esteem, perceived stress, locus of control, depression, anxiety, and attitude towards marriage and the family. Group participation was also associated with decreased levels of abuse, although these results were most likely due to the abusers' knowledge that their actions were being monitored and that in order to maintain the relationship their abuse would have to stop (at least for a while). It is unreasonable to expect any intervention with battered women to effect any cessation of abuse; only the abusers can end the cycle of violence.

TREATMENT OUTCOME STUDIES

Many articles and books exist on treatment strategies for abused women (Bowker, 1986; Brown, 1991; Deschner, 1984; Geller, 1992; Goodman, 1995; Leeder, 1994; Pressman, Cameron , & Rothery, 1989; Walker, 1994). Although many studies have surveyed the utilization of services (Bowker, 1988; Dobash & Dobash, 1987; Dutton, 1987; Gamache, Edelson, & Schock, 1988; Johnson, 1985; McEvoy, Brookings & Brown, 1983; Murty, & Roebuck, 1992; Stark & Flitcraft, 1988; Straus, 1990; US Department of Justice, 1980), few researchers have looked at the outcome of specific treatments for battered women. Only a handful of empirical studies have been conducted to determine the efficacy of treatment: four studies of shelters (Berk, Newton, & Berk, 1986; Giles-Sims, 1983; Gondolf & Fisher, 1988; Johnson, Crowley, & Sigler, 1992), two of support groups (Mancoske, Standifer, & Cauley, 1994; Tutty, Bidgood, & Rothery, 1993), and seven of conjoint/systems therapy for abused women (Deschner, McNeil, & Moore, 1986; Geller & Walsh, 1978; Harris, 1986; Klein, 1992; Loring, Clark, & Frost, 1994; Magill & Werk, 1985 ; Neidig, & Friedman, 1984).

Although individual counseling may be one of the most widely used forms of treatment used for battered women (Bowker, 1984; Frieze, Knoble, Washburn, & Zomnir, 1980; Hamilton & Coates, 1993; Pagelow, 1981, Schulman, 1979; Strube, 1988), no empirical studies have been found on outcome of individual counseling for survivors of domestic violence per se. Many case studies and anecdotal reports have been published within treatment manuals and articles (Leeder, 1994; Geller, 1982; O'Leary, Curley, Rosenbaum, & Clarke, 1985, Walker, 1994), but none provide adequate information to be aggregated for analysis. In addition, it is possible that victims of violence may be subsumed within the samples treated for depression, anxiety, or other disorders (both psychological and physical).

Marital rape is common in abusive relationships (Pagelow, 1988; Russell, 1982); however, of the studies conducted on treatment efficacy for rape victims (Cryer & Beutler, 1980; Foa, Rothbaum, Riggs, &

Murdock, 1991; Frank, Anderson, Stewart, Dancu, Hughes, & West, 1988; Resick, Jordan, Girelli, Hutter, Dvorak, 1988; Turner & Frank, 1981; Veronen & Kilpatrick, 1983), only one mentions marital rape specifically, and in that case it is as a criterion for exclusion from the study (Foa et al., 1991). Therefore, studies on effectiveness of treatment for victims of sexual assault will be omitted from this review.

Shelters

The shelter movement in the United States paralleled the women's movement of the 1970s (Walker, 1979). Over the past two decades, battered women's shelters have evolved into multi-faceted service organizations. Shelters for abused women provide a safe haven as well as counseling, advocacy, educational programs and information about various alternatives to living with violence (Pagelow, 1981; Sedlak, 1988). Reports of utilization of shelters by abused women range from 3% to 60% (Cooper-White, 1990; Horton, et al., 1988; USDHHS, 1991). Not only do abused women call upon shelters for assistance, but their families and friends, local service agencies, police, physicians, and lawyers all benefit from the information and recommendations provided by shelter staff (Murty & Roebuck, 1992). Murty and Roebuck (1992) report that 15% of the calls received at the Atlanta Council for Battered Women were from third-party callers.

Four studies have been conducted on the efficacy of battered women's shelters (Berk et al., 1986; Giles-Sims, 1983; Gondolf & Fisher, 1988; Johnson et al., 1992). Two of these studies use reduction of violence (as measured by violence experienced) as their outcome variable (Berk et al., 1986; Giles-Sims, 1983). One indirect study uses return to the abusive relationship (Johnson, et al., 1992) and one uses the decision to return to the abuser as the dependent measure (Gondolf & Fisher, 1988). Because of the nature of the research and the population under scrutiny, none of the studies reviewed used a control group or other reference group with which to compare it's findings.

Giles-Sims (1983) conducted a study of 31 battered women who were residents at a shelter. Over three quarters of the women had been hit, punched, pushed, slapped or beaten up, and more than half had been threatened with a knife or gun. One quarter of the women had been shot or stabbed by their abuser. The average age of the sample was 29 years, and 94% were Caucasian. Sixty-seven per cent of the women had at least a high school degree, and 35% were employed outside of the home. The average income for the women in this study was ≤$10,000. The women in this study had an average of 2.5 children, and had been in their abusive relationship for an average of almost six years. Sixty-one per cent of the women were married, 26% were living with a partner, and 13% were separated or divorced.

The services utilized by the women in this study include temporary protection and interim housing, support services (not defined by the author), assistance with job placement, continued education, and location of permanent housing. In addition, the author suggests that the shelter was used as a "trump card" by women for controlling the behavior of their batterers.

Twenty-four subjects (77.4%) from the original sample received follow-up interviews six-months after the initial assessment. At six months, one third of the women were still married to their abusers, 25% were separated, and 33% were divorced. In addition, 62% of the women were either employed or full-time students. Outcome in this study was measured as violence experienced. Of the women returning to their abusive relationship, 54% reported having experienced at least one incident of violence after leaving the shelter. Although over half of these subjects reported continued violence, this was a reduction from the 100% violence rate experienced by the women in the six months prior to their entering the shelter. Not returning to the relationship did not necessarily protect the women from abuse; 44% of those subjects who left their abusers reported experiencing at least one incident of violence after leaving the shelter.

Berk and his colleagues (1986) studied 155 survivors of domestic violence who used the services of shelters in Southern California over an 18-month period. The average age of the women in this study was 30 years. Over 50% were married to their abusers, and had an average of more than two children living at home. Almost three quarters of the sample were Caucasian. Most of the women had at least a high school degree, and 48% were employed outside of the home.

The researchers identified reduction of frequency and intensity of violence, operationalized as violence experienced by the women at 90 days after leaving the shelter, as their outcome measure. Several preliminary analyses indicated that shelter residents differed from non-residents on a number of abuse related variables, such as whether the victim and abuser lived together, police were involved and helpful, the victim had other places to stay, the victim was recently injured, etc.

These variables were used to construct a "propensity score" that was entered into the model along with shelter stay and previous help-seeking behaviors, defined as the number of different types of help sources contacted (e.g., shelter, police, lawyer, counselor, etc.), for predicting future violence.

The authors report that neither shelter stay nor previous help-seeking alone were predictive of future violence, but both the propensity score and the interaction between shelter stay and previous help-seeking did predict new violence. Berk and his colleagues suggest that it is not shelter stay per se that helps women to experience less violence, but rather it is the type of *action* that the women take that leads to cessation of abuse. The more different sources of assistance that women contact, the more likely they are to address all of the issues involved in changing their abusive relationship.

Gondolf & Fisher (1988) studied over 6,000 women who used the services of 50 battered women's shelters throughout the state of Texas over an 18-month period. The women in this study were either residents of one of the shelters, or participants in of one of the non-residents' programs. All of the subjects had experienced some form of physical abuse. Approximately half of the sample had at least a high school degree (56%), had two or more children (63%), or were in the abusive relationship for one to five years (48%). Almost all of the women (90%) had very low annual incomes (≤$10,000). More than half of the women were Caucasian (57%), 29% were Hispanic, and 15% were African-American.

The researchers analyzed the shelter residents separately from the non-residents on the variables related to the decision to return to the abuser. While the sample size for this analysis is not specified in the text, Gondolf and Fisher report that shelter residents used the following services: 85% used counseling, 73% used transportation , 67% used referral, 25% used child care and counseling, 24% used legal assistance, and 19% used employment assistance.

Outcome was measured at the end of the residents stay at the shelter. The length of stay (and therefore the follow-up period) was not specified by the authors. The decision to return to the abuser was measured by planned living arrangements after leaving the shelter. Twenty-four per cent of the residents reported that they planned to return to their abuser. Of the 75% who did not plan to return, 30% planned to live with relatives, 17% with friends, and 29% on their own. The researchers also looked at variables related to the subjects' decision-making. The most influential predictors of outcome were whether the woman's batterer was in counseling (-.57), she had her own transportation (.50), there was affordable child care available to her (.49), and she had her own income (.31).

In an indirect study of shelter effectiveness, Johnson et al. (1992), surveyed 11 domestic violence shelters in Alabama. The shelters were asked to identify the components of their resident and non-resident programs, and to report the results of their resident follow-up surveys. These domestic violence programs consisted of safe interim housing, referrals to other public service agencies for assistance with employment, education and housing, counseling, legal advocates, and children's services.

The purpose and objective of the shelter programs were to end the abuse by helping the residents to become self-sufficient. Success of shelter programs was measured by the proportion of former residents who were able to leave their batterers. At follow-up (interval not specified by the authors), the shelter staff reported that 50% of the residents had not returned to their abusive relationships.

Although each of these studies appears to indicate that shelter programs were somewhat effective in helping battered women, methodological inadequacies and variations between studies preclude the drawing of any conclusions about shelter effectiveness.

Support Groups

Support groups are essentially self-help groups, although they are usually led by someone with counseling training. Often the facilitator or a co-facilitator is a survivor of domestic violence (Donato & Bowker, 1984; Tutty, et al., 1993). Support groups are considered the treatment of choice for abused women by many practitioners (Bowker & Maurer, 1986; Donato & Bowker, 1984; Pagelow, 1981; Tutty, et al., 1993; Walker, 1979). Support groups offer women the opportunity to share their experiences of living with domestic violence. In addition, group facilitators provide education and information about domestic violence as well as referrals to other community resources (e.g., legal services, counselors, and children's services). Most support groups are open to new members each week (i. e., "drop-in" group membership) and are time unlimited.

Several studies indicate that women's groups are not one of the most commonly contacted resources, despite the fact that they provided some of the most specialized services for abused women (Bowker & Maurer, 1986; Donato & Bowker, 1984; Hamilton & Coates, 1993; Pagelow, 1981; Tutty, et al., 1993; Walker, 1979). It is estimated that fewer than 25% of battered women attend support groups as a method for dealing with domestic violence (Bowker & Maurer, 1986; Donato & Bowker, 1984).

There are two outcome studies of support group programs for adult survivors of domestic violence (Mancoske, Standifer, & Cauley, 1994; Tutty, Bidgood, & Rothery, 1993). Both of these studies utilize a pre-test/post-test questionnaire design for assessing subject change. Although the studies identify similar theoretical concepts as the basis for assessing efficacy of the groups (e.g., self-esteem, self-efficacy, etc.), each of the studies uses different criteria and measurement tools. One of the studies (Mancoske et al., 1994) compares two types of group treatment, but neither uses a control group for comparative purposes.

Tutty et al. (1993) conducted a study on the effectiveness of 12 support groups in Canada. They surveyed 76 women prior to starting group participation. The groups met weekly for 10 to 12 weeks, and each session lasted two to three hours. Sixty of the participants (79%) were tested upon completion of the program, and 32 (42%)were surveyed again at six-months to assess for longer term results. The goals of the group program were to decrease isolation and stress, increase self-esteem and self-efficacy, provide education regarding abuse and family relations. In addition, the overall purpose of the group was to assist the participants in experiencing less abuse. Ten instruments were used to measure the subjects' levels of social support, locus of control, self-esteem, perceived stress/coping, attitudes towards marriage and the family, marital relations, history of abuse, conflict management, and satisfaction with the group. In addition, group leaders were asked to make a corresponding clinical judgment (using a behaviorally anchored four-point Likert scale questionnaire) of client functioning for every outcome measure completed by the clients.

The average age of the group participants was 35 years. Almost all of the women (91%) had children, most having at least two living at home. Fifty-four per cent were married or cohabitating, and 38% were separated or divorced. The subjects had an average annual income of $14,600. The racial/ethnic and educational background of the sample was not included by the authors. All of the group members had experienced some physical or verbal abuse during the month preceding their group participation, 11% reported receiving physical violence requiring medical attention. The participants did not demonstrate a more external locus of control, nor more traditional attitudes toward marriage and the family relative to population norms; however, the women were characterized by low self-esteem and clinical levels of marital dysfunction as well as violence.

Upon completion of group participation, significant change in the hypothesized direction was reported for the following variables: locus of control, self-esteem, perceived stress/coping, attitudes towards marriage and the family, and marital relations. In addition, the subjects' reported decreases in receipt of physical and non-physical abuse, and controlling behavior; however only one of the subjects' (4%) reported complete cessation of physical violence. There were significant positive changes on the following variables at the 6-month follow-up for the 32 women remaining in the sample: self-esteem, perceived stress/coping, attitudes towards marriage and the family, martial relations, and receipt of physical abuse and controlling behavior. Due to the relatively small sample size, these findings should be interpreted with caution.

The authors state that the therapist ratings provided corroborating evidence for a number of variables on which the subjects had documented significant improvement (without specifying those variables), except for receipt of physical and verbal abuse and controlling behavior. Finally, 87% of the women reported that the program had met most or all of their needs. The authors suggest that the all of the gains reported by the subjects' except for receipt of abuse and controlling behavior can be associated with support group content. However, the researchers conclude that the decreased levels of abuse and controlling behaviors may have been due to the fact that the subjects' abusive partners were aware that their behaviors were under scrutiny from an external source, and that interventions for the victims of abuse do not in and of themselves result in cessation of violence.

Mancoske et al. (1994) examined the effectiveness of two types of ¬oort groups for battered women, using a comparative treatment pre-ⁿt-test groups design. Twenty women requesting counseling services through a battered women's program in Louisiana were assigned to one of two short-term support/counseling groups—feminist oriented or a grief resolution oriented. Each group met weekly for eight weeks. All sessions were provided by one of two graduate students in social work. In addition, all of the women received brief crisis intervention services, including assessment of imminent danger, education on abuse, information on community resources and planning for safety.

All of the subjects had experienced some form of abuse in the six-months prior to joining the group; 65% reporting abuse within the previous month. Ninety per cent had been both physically and non-physically abused, with the remainder of the sample receiving only verbal/psychological abuse. Sixty per cent of the subjects were married, 30% were single, and 10% were divorced. Almost half of the women (40%) had been in the abusive relationship less than five years, and 65% were still living with their abuser. The average number of children was reported to be 2.25. The subjects' average age was 28.5 years. Sixty-five percent of the sample was Caucasian, and 30% African-American. Half of the women had at least a high school degree, and 75% reported an annual income of less than $10,000.

The researchers selected self-esteem, self-efficacy, and attitudes toward feminism as their measures of change. Overall, the women who participated in the group program reported significant improvements in self-esteem, self-efficacy, and feminist attitudes. When examining differential treatment outcomes between the groups, the authors report that the women who attended the grief resolution group showed increases in self-esteem and self-efficacy, but not feminist attitudes, while those women attending the feminist group did not show statistically significant improvements on any of the variables. This study offers some evidence of the improved outcomes in group work with battered women, but the results of this study should be interpreted with caution due to the very small sample size.

While these studies suggest that support programs were somewhat effective in helping battered women, methodological inadequacies and the paucity of research preclude any inferences about support group program effectiveness in general.

Conjoint Counseling

Conjoint counseling, or couples' therapy, is used selectively with couples who have indicated a commitment to cease physical abuse and work on improving the relationship. Family therapists agree that couples' therapy should be used only when the victim did not want to leave the relationship (Margolin, 1993). All of the studies reviewed cited contraindications for use of couples' therapy. These contraindications include the lack of commitment by the batterer to cease the violence, concomitant substance abuse, and severity of violence (e.g., continued danger to the victim). The purpose of conjoint therapy is to expedite the cessation of violence by treating both the abused and the abuser within the context of the relationship. In some models of couples' therapy, the batterer takes the ultimate responsibility for the abuse, but in others, the violence is seen from an interactional perspective and both members of the couple are seen as victims. Formats for conjoint treatment vary from structured dyadic to group counseling sessions; most are cognitive-behavioral, with an emphasis on communication and decision-making skills training, and enhancing intimacy (Deschner, et al. 1986, Margolin, 1979; Neidig & Friedman, 1984).

Proponents of conjoint treatment for spouse abuse argue that the majority of battered women want to stay their relationships, without the violence (Geller & Walsh, 1979; Geller, 1992), but no estimates exist on the percentage of abusive couples seeking conjoint therapy.

Marital researchers and clinicians have conducted seven studies of conjoint/systems therapy for abused women (Deschner, McNeil, & Moore, 1986; Geller & Walsh, 1978; Harris, 1986; Klein, 1992; Loring, Clark, & Frost, 1994; Magill & Werk, 1985 ; Neidig, & Friedman, 1984). All of the these studies except one (Loring, et al., 1994) identified cessation of violence as their primary measure of outcome. Loring and her colleagues studied the effectiveness of treatment for emotionally abused women, and defined outcome as cessation of verbal/psychological abuse, rather than physical violence.

Geller and Walsh (1978) report on a model of conjoint treatment ~ed to violent couples seen at a victims' information bureau in New ~te. The brief report does not include the number of couples ~rogram, but describes the sample as almost exclusively ~ median income of $12,000. The average age of the couples was 35 years. The couples had been married an average of 15 years, and the relationship had been abusive for almost as long as they had been married in 90% of the couples.

The form of therapy evaluated in this study consisted of getting the abuser to agree to stop the violence, behavioral anger management interventions with the abuser, and communications and problem-solving skills training. The duration and specifics of the therapy are not described by the authors.

The researchers assert that their program had proven to be effective because the clients report "feeling less isolated" and having a "better sense of self" after therapy. In addition, Geller and Walsh claim that every couple involved in the program for a minimum of three weeks had experienced a cessation of violence, and that two thirds of the couples had remained in the program longer than the three week minimum. Because of the lack of clear objectives, descriptions and methods of this study, the accuracy of the results cannot be verified.

In Neidig and Friedman (1984), the authors report the success of their approach to treating marital violence in a military setting (Neidig, Friedman, & Howell, unpublished manuscript). The goal of their small group couples' therapy was to eliminate violence in the relationship. The program focused on the abuser, but included dyadic exercises designed to enhance positive interactions between the spouses. Behavioral interventions used for the battered included contracting to stop violence, learning to use time-outs and other anger management techniques. The couples received treatment designed to enhance problem-solving and communication skills, and increase positive interactions. The authors do not provide a description of the same, and the original source is no longer available.

The researchers assessed the couples' history of violence and conflict management, relationship functioning, individual functioning, and current life events during an intake interview prior to beginning treatment. The couples were reassessed upon completion of the program and at 6-months. Neidig and Friedman state that 80% of the program participants reported no violence at the 6-month follow-up. The lack of details on the methodology employed at follow-up and specificity of the sample precludes judgment on the results of this study.

In a pilot project designed to evaluate the efficacy of couples' therapy for ending domestic violence, Magill and Werk (1985) studie

25 couples at a marital violence clinic in Canada. The therapy included crisis intervention, behavioral treatment in how to identify cues that contribute to angry interactions, establish ground rules that prohibit violence, interrupt pattern of conflict, and increase positive interactions between the partners. The couples met with the counselors on a weekly basis for two to nine months. No descriptive information on the sample was provided by the authors.

Assessments of marital functioning and history of abuse were conducted during the first interview and upon completion of treatment. The researchers report that at follow-up, only one of the couples had experienced a recurrence of physical violence. The authors conclude that these results are "encouraging" and that they were conducting "more extensive evaluative outcome research."

Harris (1986) developed a program that combined individual and conjoint counseling for abusive couples. The overall goal of the therapy was to stop future violence from occurring. Using a cognitive-behavioral model, initial individual sessions were used to educate each member of the couple about the cycle of violence, anger and conflict management techniques, and to assess the level of violence experienced. Conjoint sessions, started after completion of the initial individual sessions, were led by male and female co-therapists. The goal of the conjoint therapy was to recognize and change behavior patterns, and to learn and practice new communication and problem-solving skills.

Forty case files were randomly selected from over 200 couples completing the treatment program over a five year period. The average age of the male partners was 32.5 years, and of the females was 30 years. The couples had been together an average of six years, with over half (63%) reporting violence from early in the relationship. Sixty percent of the couples reported experiencing violence less than once per month, making this a comparatively non-violent group. Sixty-three percent of the couples were married, and 14% were either separated or divorced. The average income for the couples was just over $18,000. The couples attended an average of five counseling sessions (range = 2-

interviews were conducted on all 40 couples to assess for 'erity of abuse, as well as overall relationship and 'ing. Follow-up assessments were conducted on 30 'd between the end of treatment and the follow-up varied from two months to three years. Of the 30 couples contacted at follow-up, 22 (73%) reported cessation of violent behaviors. The authors report several client/couple factors associated with treatment outcome: age of batterer, income, onset of violence, and number of counseling sessions attended. The couples reporting successful outcome were older, had higher incomes, later onset of violence, and had attended more sessions. The variation in follow-up, along with other factors (e.g., lack of specificity about methodology, small sample size, etc.), make interpretation of the study results difficult.

Deschner et al. (1986) evaluated a group treatment model of anger management for couples. The purpose of the treatment was to eliminate violence in the relationship. In a ten week program, couples met weekly for 2a hours to learn about time-outs, the effects of diet on behavior, stress management, cognitive restructuring, listening and assertiveness, and problem-solving.

Forty-seven couples were assessed upon completing the program (no sample characteristics were reported). Significant improvements were reported in number of arguments per week, level of anger during arguments, and marital happiness. Slight (not statistically significant) improvements were reported in number of violent incidents per week, perhaps due to low base rates. Fifteen of the couples were surveyed at eight months post-treatment. Eight couples reported no further violence, and five couples reported engaging in "minor physical incidents" (e.g., grabbing or slapping). Based on this information, the authors conclude that "87 percent of those reached had avoided further battering." The researchers obviously do not consider grabbing or slapping to be physical violence; however, using outcome criteria from the other studies reviewed, only 53% of a very small sample (the 15 couples followed-up at eight months) were successful in eliminating violence from their relationships.

Klein (1992) conducted a study to compare the effectiveness of two treatment approaches to domestic violence. Conjoint group treatment was compared with a group program for the abusers only. The participants were 57 male spouses on active military duty who were identified as having committed at least one act of physical violence against their wives during a one year period. Thirty of the subjects and their wives were assigned to receive conjoint counseling, while 27 of the men were assigned to the male-only group treatment.

The groups met one a week for 10 weeks, and consisted of behavioral treatment to increase communication, problem-solving, and anger management skills. The author reports that no significant differences were found between the two approaches; both were effective in significantly reducing physical violence. At two-month follow-up, 80% of both the abusers and their wives reported a cessation of physical abuse; however an equal percentage of the sample reported continued verbal/psychological abuse during the same period. Care must be taken when interpreting these results. The details of the follow-up assessments are not provided by the authors. If the follow-up was conducted in the presence of both members of the couple, it is possible that the self-reported cessation of physical violence was due to demand characteristics and the victims fear of reprisal rather than actual change in behavior.

In the only study of therapy for non-physically abused women, Loring and her colleagues (1994) evaluated a combination of individual and conjoint treatment. The goal of the treatment was to eliminate emotional abuse within the relationship. The therapy consisted of weekly individual sessions and three conjoint sessions, each lasting one to two hours. The content of the sessions included recognizing patterns of abuse, teaching the victim to emotionally disattach from the abuser, and increasing individual self-efficacy and positive dyadic interactions.

Eighty-seven emotionally abused women and their abusers from the Atlanta area participated in the treatment. None of the women reported physical abuse in the relationship, which ranged from one to 34 years in length. The age of the women ranged from 17 to 83 years; 59% were Caucasian, 36% were African-American, and 5% were Hispanic. It is unclear how and when the couple were assessed. The authors report that 76 (87%) of the women described "increased closeness in the relationship" and in increased ability to recognize their "tendency to minimize the impact of emotional abuse." The results of this study are unclear due to lack of specific outcome criteria and methods of assessment.

Although comparing the outcome of these studies is difficult due to methodological inconsistencies, several commonalties are apparent. First, it appears that conjoint therapy is not recommended for a certain type of couples. Couples with frequent and severe levels of violence, and those in which the batterer is a substance abuser and/or unwilling to change are not appropriate candidates for conjoint treatment. In addition, five of the seven studies reviewed (Geller & Walsh, 1978; Harris, 1986; Klein, 1992; Magill & Werk, 1985; Neidig, & Friedman, 1984) followed similar treatment and assessment protocols. These studies indicate that for the subset of abusive couples appropriate for conjoint treatment, cognitive-behavioral therapy may be somewhat effective in reducing or eliminating physical violence. However, further research must be conducted, using standardized methodology and outcome measures, before more definitive conclusions can be drawn.

STUDY RATIONALE

As is evident from the studies reviewed above, research on the effectiveness of programs and services for abused women is lacking in systematic methodology. This poses problems to both researchers and service providers. Using a wide variety of outcome criteria and measures limits the comparability and generalizability of research findings. This lack of systematic assessment also does not assist community service, medical, and mental health providers, and ultimately the battered women whom they serve. Poor research and/or contradictory findings do not lead to improvement in, or adoption of, the services available to abused women. Carefully conducted, systematic research should inform practice and enable service providers to enhance the quality of care they provide.

The purpose of this study was to explore not only the utilization of services by battered women, but also to systematically assess the efficacy of a specific type of service (i.e., community support groups), and to compare the perceived helpfulness of commonly used community and professional services for abused women.

In addition, research on the effects of non-physical forms of abuse is rare, and no one has, to date, evaluated and compared the harmfulness of physical versus non-physical abuse. Therefore, this study attempted to measure and compare the perceived harmfulness of four types of abuse: physical, sexual, verbal, and psychological, and to explore the effects of that abuse on battered women's levels of depression, anxiety and self-esteem.

In order to increase the generalizability of the findings, both support group participants and crisis line callers were surveyed. However, due to time constraints and safety issues, crisis line callers were surveyed only regarding service utilization and overall helpfulness. Support group participants were surveyed in greater detail about perceived helpfulness, and were given a complete battery of assessments regarding history of abuse, and current depression, anxiety, and self-esteem.

SPECIFIC AIMS

The purpose of this study was to assess the adequacy and efficacy of community and professional services used by battered women. This study examined the utilization and perceived effectiveness of services offered by a local battered women's shelter and agency, and other community and professional services available to abused women in Western and Central Oregon.

In addition, this study examined psychological and social correlates of abuse among battered women who seek help. The type and amount of abuse experienced by a group of help-seeking abused women was assessed. In addition, the women rated how much each type of abuse hurt them. Finally, the women's levels of depression, anxiety, and self-esteem were examined in order to determine the relation between different types of abuse and the mental health consequences of domestic violence.

An additional purpose of this study was to assemble a battery of reliable and valid measures for use in domestic violence research in order to provide researchers with a methodology to determine dependent variables relevant to the study of domestic violence.

- The primary aim was to examine the usage and perceived helpfulness of community support groups, counselors/therapists, physicians, lawyers, clergy, police, and family members by abused women. Therefore, support group participants and crisis line callers were assessed for demographic characteristics, level of community/professional resource usage, and overall satisfaction ratings. Support group participants were also asked to identify specifically what they found to be helpful about the services that they used. A comparison of support group participants and crisis line callers was conducted to assess for differences in service utilization and perceived effectiveness.

- A secondary aim of this study was to collect information about the type and severity of abuse experienced by women seeking the services of a domestic violence agency. The type and frequency of abuse were assessed, as well as the subjects' perceived harmfulness ratings of that abuse.

- An additional aim of this study was to conduct exploratory investigations of the relation between domestic abuse and the levels of depression, anxiety, and self-esteem among participants of the support groups.

Method

DOMESTIC VIOLENCE SERVICES IN OREGON

There are approximately 25 agencies throughout Oregon that provide support group services. This study collected information from agencies who used the services of three domestic violence agencies in Oregon and Oregon... Women come... to agencies, the Center Against Rape and Domestic Violence in Corvallis, and the Center... Womenspace and Hope Alliance in Bend.

Domestic violence agencies in Oregon provide comprehensive services to women and children fleeing domestic violence. The mission of these agencies is to empower women and children to take control of their lives. They provide a safe and secure environment in which to socialize their options. Staff and volunteers assist battered women to rebuild their self-confidence and to make the positive changes necessary to establish a violence-free life. Domestic violence agencies work to eliminate the cycle of violence by providing a wide range of services designed to meet the varying needs of their clients.

Distinct programs include a 24-hour Crisis Line, a 24-hour emergency Shelter Program with support services, Drop-in Community Support Groups, Community Education Programs, and transitional programs. From August 1993 through July 1994, Womenspace, the domestic violence agency serving Lane County in Western Oregon, provided emergency shelter and services to 616 women and children and received over 5,000 crisis and information line calls. During a 24-hour period of work, staff and 142 volunteers received longer-term services through the agency's programs.

Method

DOMESTIC VIOLENCE SERVICES IN OREGON

There are approximately 25 agencies throughout Oregon that provide support group services. This study collected information from abused women who used the services of three domestic violence agencies in Western and Central Oregon: Womenspace in Eugene, the Center Against Rape and Domestic Violence in Corvallis, and the Central Oregon Battering and Rape Alliance in Bend.

Domestic violence agencies in Oregon provide comprehensive services to women and children fleeing domestic violence. The mission of these agencies is to empower women and children to take control of their lives. They provide a safe and secure environment in which to consider their options. Staff and volunteers assist battered women to regain their self confidence and to make the positive changes necessary to maintain a violence-free life. Domestic violence agencies work to interrupt the cycle of violence by providing a wide range of services designed to meet the varying needs of their clients.

Typical programs include a 24-hour Crisis Line, a 24-hour Emergency Shelter Program with support services, Drop-in Community Support Groups, Community Education Programs, and transitional programs. From August 1993 through July 1994, Womenspace, the domestic violence agency serving Lane County, in Western Oregon, provided emergency shelter and services to 616 women and children, and received over 3,000 crisis and information request calls. During the same period, 52 women and 142 children received longer term services in their transitional programs.

Support group programs provide women with the opportunity to share their experiences with peers. Trained volunteers facilitate both drop-in (open to all women) and closed (open only to specific populations of women) support groups located in urban and rural settings throughout Western and Central Oregon. Approximately 750 women were served by the support groups in Lane County alone between June 1, 1993 and May 31, 1994.

Community support groups are open to all women, many of whom are referred by Crisis Line volunteers, social service agencies, criminal justice system workers, psychologists and counselors. The groups are offered both during the day and in the evenings, and are approximately two hours in length. Free child care is provided to group participants. Support groups work to interrupt the cycle of violence through education, emotional support, and information exchange. The content of the groups typically includes: education about the nature of domestic violence and alternatives to living with abuse; exercises and other efforts to build self confidence and self-esteem, and; individual sharing of experience and group discussion to reduce isolation and promote problem solving.

Support group facilitators are usually volunteers with a minimum of one year experience with direct client service (e.g., crisis line, advocacy, etc.), and some experience in leading groups, or counselors specializing in treatment of domestic violence. In Lane County, facilitators of Womenspace support groups must attend 14 hours of general training, 15 hours of training in their service area, and specific training in facilitating domestic violence support groups. In addition, facilitators receive ongoing in-service training, provided by Womenspace staff, personnel from other agencies, and mental health professionals.

Group facilitators collect limited statistical information about group attendance and child care utilization. This information includes: the number of individual women attending the group; the number of times those women attend during the month; number of times children have attended child care; number of volunteers, and; total number of volunteer hours for the month. This information has been used by the Director and staff of Womenspace for funding purposes. No other information has been collected on the community support groups.

Domestic violence agencies have identified general goals and outcomes for their support group programs. Their primary goals for the support groups are to provide education about domestic abuse, encourage information sharing/problem-solving, provide a safe environment to share personal experiences, encourage relationship formation with others, encourage peer support, provide child care to give women a break, facilitate empowerment of women, validate their experiences, build social skills, enhance social/recreational life, educate women in how government/criminal justice system operates, and educate women in how to make social change to end domestic violence.

SUBJECTS

One hundred-thirty two subjects from Western and Central Oregon were recruited from six community support groups in three counties, and from callers to the Womenspace 24-hour Crisis Line in Eugene, Oregon. The subjects were eligible for participation in the study if they had ever experienced physical or psychological abuse by an intimate partner. Sixty-six support group participants and 66 crisis line callers completed the questionnaires. All of the subjects were women.

Combined Sample

The combined sample consisted of 66 support group participants and 66 crisis line callers. The total sample had a mean age of 37. Seventy percent of the women were not living with abuser at the time they completed the survey. Fifty-one percent were married or living with partner, and 47% were single or divorced.

Table 1. Combined Sample: Age, Income, Relationship Length, and Separation Length

Variable	N	Mean	SD
Age	130	37.25	10.13
Income	131	$13689.42	13277.80
Relationship Length (in years)	129	8.69	8.82
Separation Length (in years)	91	1.78	3.69
No. of Resources Used	132	4.65	1.87

The subjects reported an average length of 9 years for the abusive relationship. Those women who were separated from their abusers reported an average length of 1.8 years of separation.

Table 2. Combined Sample: Demographic Characteristics

Variable	Frequency	Percent
Race/Ethnicity		
Caucasian	113	85.6
Native American	8	6.1
Hispanic/Latino	7	5.3
African-American	2	1.5
Asian	1	.8
Other	1	.8
Education		
0-8	5	3.8
9-11	10	7.6
High School	32	24.2
Some College	55	41.7
College Grad	16	12.1
Post College	9	6.8
Employment		
Full-Time	26	19.7
Part-Time	30	22.7
Homemaker	51	38.6
Student	8	6.1
Unemployed	15	11.4
Insurance		
Yes	95	72.0
Marital Status		
Single/Divorced	62	47.0
Married	52	39.4
Living with Partner	15	11.4
Live with Abuser		
Yes	38	28.8
No	92	69.7
Children Live With		
Yes	73	55.3

Sixty-one percent of the sample had attended at least some college. Forty-three percent of the women were employed outside of the home full or part time, and 39% reported being full time homemakers. Fifty-five percent of the women had children living at home. The average income was $13,700.00, with a median income of $9,600.00. Eight-six percent of the sample was Caucasian, 6% Native American, 5% Hispanic/Latino, and the remainder of was comprised of African-American, Asian & other. Seventy-two percent reported having some form of insurance (including the Oregon Health Plan for low income families). The women who participated in this study reported having contacted an average of 4.65 community/professional resources. Age, income, relationship length, and separation length for the combined sample are presented in Table 1. Other characteristics of the combined sample are presented in Table 2.

Support Group Sample

The support group sample had a mean age of 37.5. Eighty-five percent of the women were not living with abuser at the time they completed the survey. Sixty-one percent were single or divorced. The subjects reported an average length of 9 years for the abusive relationship. Those women who were separated from their abusers reported an average length of 1.6 years of separation.

Table 3. Support Group Sample: Age, Income, Relationship Length, Separation Length, and Number of Resources Used

Variable	N	Mean	SD
Age	65	37.57	10.82
Income	65	$12593.11	12133.90
Relationship Length (in years)	64	9.11	9.82
Separation Length (in years)	55	1.59	2.60
No. of Resources Used	66	5.64	1.63

Sixty-eight percent of the sample had attended at least some college. Fifty percent of the women were employed outside of the home full or part time, and 38% reported being full time homemakers.

Fifty-five percent of the women had children living at home. The average income was $12,600.00, with a median income of $8,450.00. Eight percent of the sample was Caucasian, 12% Native American, 6% Hispanic/Latino, and the remainder of was comprised of other non-specified groups.

Table 4. Support Group Sample: Demographic Characteristics

Variable	Frequency	Percent
Race/Ethnicity		
Caucasian	53	80.3
Native American	8	12.1
Hispanic/Latino	4	6.1
Other	1	1.5
Education		
9-11	3	4.5
High School	18	27.3
Some College	30	45.5
College Grad	11	16.7
Post College	4	6.1
Employment		
Full-Time	14	21.2
Part-Time	19	28.8
Homemaker	25	37.9
Student	5	7.6
Unemployed	1	1.5
Insurance		
Yes	52	78.8
No	14	21.2
Marital Status		
Single/Divorced	40	60.6
Married	21	31.8
Living with Partner	5	7.6
Live with Abuser		
Yes	10	15.2
No	56	84.8
Children Live With		
Yes	36	54.5
No	20	30.3

Seventy-nine percent of the sample reported having some form of insurance (including the Oregon Health Plan for low income families). The support group subjects reported using a mean of 5.6 different types of community and professional resources.

In addition to demographics, support group participants provided information on a variety of other variables. Number of children, number of abusers, number of leave attempts, Number of time attend groups, amount of total abuse, amounts of abuse by type, BAI, BDI, and RSE. Support group sample characteristics are presented in Table 3 and Table 4.

Crisis Line Sample

The crisis line sample had a mean age of 37. Fifty-five percent of the women were not living with abuser at the time they completed the survey. Sixty-two percent were married or living with a partner, and 33% were single or divorced. The subjects reported an average length of 8 years for the abusive relationship. Those women who were separated from their abusers reported an average length of 2.1 years of separation.

Table 5. Crisis Line Sample: Age, Income, Relationship Length, Separation Length, and Number of Resources Used

Variable	N	Mean	SD
Age	65	36.92	9.47
Income	66	$14769.12	14326.47
Relationship Length (in years)	65	8.28	7.77
Separation Length (in years)	36	2.07	4.95
No. of Resources Used	66	3.67	1.54

Fifty-six percent of the sample had attended at least some college. Thirty-five percent of the women were employed outside of the home full or part time, and 39% reported being full time homemakers. Fifty-six percent of the women had children living at home. The average income was $14,800.00, with a median income of $10,500.00.

Table 6. Crisis Line Sample: Demographic Characteristics

Variable	Frequency	Percent
Race/Ethnicity		
Caucasian	60	90.9
Hispanic/Latino	3	4.5
African-American	2	3.0
Asian	1	1.5
Education		
0-8	5	7.6
9-11	7	10.6
High School	14	21.2
Some College	25	37.9
College Grad	5	7.6
Post College	5	7.6
Employment		
Full-Time	12	18.2
Part-Time	11	16.7
Homemaker	26	39.4
Student	3	4.5
Unemployed	14	21.2
Insurance		
Yes	43	65.2
No	22	33.3
Marital Status		
Single/Divorced	22	33.3
Married	31	47.0
Living with Partner	10	15.2
Live with Abuser		
Yes	28	42.4
No	36	54.5
Children Live With		
Yes	37	56.1
No	27	40.9

Ninety-one percent of the sample was Caucasian, 4.5% Hispanic/Latino, 3% African-American, and 1.5% Asian. Sixty-five percent reported having some form of insurance (including the Oregon Health Plan for low income families). The crisis line callers reported having contacted an average of 3.67

community and professional resources. Crisis line sample characteristics are presented in Table 5 and Table 6.

COMPARISON OF CRISIS LINE SURVEY RESPONDENTS TO ALL CRISIS LINE CALLERS

Between January 1, and May 31, 1996, the crisis line received over 1,000 crisis calls and 400 information referral calls. Table 7 contains a complete list of calls per month by type of call. About one third of the crisis calls were from women in imminent danger or extreme emotional distress, which excluded them from participating in the study, leaving a approximately 1,100 eligible callers. Approximately 25 percent of these calls were from repeat callers, leaving a total of 825 callers. The 66 surveys collected represents 8% of the total number of eligible callers.

Table 7. Womenspace Crisis Line Summary: Number of Calls per Month by Type of Call

Type of Call	1/96	2/96	3/96	4/96	5/96
Crisis	300	185	161	200	226
Information/Referral	140	66	55	58	80

DESIGN

This study used a quasi-experimental design, and a multi-method approach for data collection. This approach included gathering both quantitative and qualitative information on the community support group program. Perceived effectiveness of community and professional resources was collected via written and phone surveys of two samples of abused women. In addition, types and severity of abuse, and its psychosocial correlates were gathered via support group participants' self-reported ratings on standardized measures. Support group participants also provided feedback regarding the quality of the support group program and made suggestions for program improvement via open-ended questions on the support group survey.

DATA COLLECTION TECHNIQUES

Separate questionnaires were developed for support group facilitators, participants, and crisis line callers to collect demographic information (e.g., age, socioeconomic status, racial/ethnic group, education level, etc.), and to assess the perceived helpfulness of community and professional services for abused women. Other questionnaires were developed in order to gather more detailed information about the support groups from participants. In addition, extant questionnaires were used to assess for the following support group participant characteristics: type, frequency and perceived harmfulness of abuse received, perceived self-esteem, and current levels of depression and anxiety.

The participant questionnaires were distributed from September 1995 through May 1996. All women attending community support groups and selected callers to the crisis line were invited to participate in the study. To increase the response rate of the participants, $10.00 was offered to each support group participant returning completed questionnaires. At the end of each session, the support group participants were asked to complete five questionnaires which took approximately 40 minutes to complete. Sixty-six women (out of approximately 82 support group participants) completed the support group survey; of those, 63 completed all five surveys. Approximately 13 women were unable to participate due to scheduling conflicts, and 3 women refused to participate (approximately 20% of the total group participants).

Crisis line data collection began in January of 1996. Crisis line volunteers were offered three training sessions in conducting phone interviews. Approximately 15 volunteers attended at least one of the training sessions. Each training session was approximately 20-30 minutes in length, and covered the study purpose, criteria for participation in the study, description of survey, and brief instruction in telephone interview techniques.

The crisis line survey was offered to selected survivors of domestic violence who called the Womenspace crisis line between January 1, 1996 and May 31, 1996. Victims of domestic violence who called for information, referrals, or crisis counseling were asked to complete a telephone survey. Callers were not asked to participate if they were in immediate danger of harm, in extreme emotional crisis, or were not themselves victims of domestic violence (e.g., family members or friends of a victim). Crisis line callers were not paid for their participation. The survey was collected at the end of the call and took approximately five minutes to complete. Sixty-six women completed the crisis line survey. The crisis line received over 1,400 crisis calls between January 1, 1996 and May 31, 1996. Of those calls, 825 women were eligible for participation in the study. Due to difficulties with phone volunteers collecting data, only 8% of crisis line callers completed surveys.

CRISIS LINE VOLUNTEER CRITERIA FOR SUBJECT SELECTION

An informal interview of a random sample of crisis line volunteers was conducted to determine the criteria used by the volunteers to select which callers received/did not receive the survey. Crisis line volunteers had great difficulty collecting surveys. Volunteer identified several obstacles that impeded their ability to conduct the phone surveys. First, many volunteers were new and had just received their training. Trying to collect survey data was too much for them to do in addition to learning how to counsel crisis callers and provide information and referrals to other community services. Many volunteers also stated that they felt uncomfortable asking callers to complete a survey after the caller was "finished" discussing her issues.

In addition, the volunteers had difficulty identifying which type of caller to survey. Many volunteers did not attend any of the training sessions and were not aware that any woman who had been a victim of domestic violence (including those women who were calling for information or referrals) was eligible to participate. Many volunteers thought that only women calling for crisis counseling (i.e., women who were calling to discuss their abusive situation, not to ask for information or resource referrals) were eligible, which directly conflicted with the written criteria listed on the survey phone script. Therefore, these volunteers collected no surveys.

Finally, the most salient reason that volunteers did not conduct phone surveys was lack of time. Crisis line workers not only answer crisis calls, they must also field information and referral questions, answer calls regarding donations and other business matters, and take messages for staff and residents of the shelter. The volunteers are responsible for answering three phone lines to a busy battered women's shelter. Thus, the only way data collection became viable was for the researcher to assist in conducting the phone surveys. The additional person made it possible for both volunteer and researcher to collect data. The researcher and those phone volunteers who asked callers if they would complete a survey reported that all of the women they asked agreed to participate in the study. Therefore, if more callers were given the opportunity to participate, much more data could have been collected.

MEASURES

Measures of Community and Professional Services

The Support Group Survey (SGS)

The SGS is a 60-item self-report measure for participants of community support group programs. The SGS was developed by the researcher to gather quantitative and qualitative information from the participants about their experiences with the support groups. The SGS was designed to collect demographic data about the participants, quantitative data about the groups' perceived usefulness, and qualitative suggestions for program improvement. This measure was pilot-tested (for both content and process) with a small sample (n=10) of ex-participants from several battered women's support groups and women selected at random from the Eugene/Springfield area. This measure was designed for and tested by women with a wide range of reading abilities. In addition to pilot testing, this measure was reviewed by staff at a local domestic violence agency for appropriateness and validity of the content. Reliability analyses on the measure produced inter-item correlations ranging from .50 to .62. The test-retest reliability is approximately .91, based on a small subsample (n=5) who completed the measure a second time between 1 and 5 months after the initial testing. A copy of the SGS is contained in Appendix A.

The Crisis Line Survey

The Crisis Line Survey (CLS) is a 28-item phone interview questionnaire. The CLS was developed by the researcher to gather a subset of questions from the PSGS from callers to the Womenspace Crisis Line. The CLS contains a subset of demographic items from the PSGS, plus questions designed to assess community and professional resource usage and the perceived helpfulness of those services. This measure was reviewed by the staff at a local domestic violence agency for appropriateness and validity of the content. A copy of the CLS is contained in Appendix A.

Measures of Abuse

The Inventory of Abuse (IA)

The Inventory of Abuse (IA) is a shortened version of the 60-item Measure for Wife Abuse developed by Rodenburg and Fantuzzo (1993) to assess a broad range of abusive behaviors. The Measure for Wife Abuse was selected for use in this study over more traditional measures (e.g., the Conflict Tactics Scale, Straus 1979) because it measures four types of abuse using very detailed questions, and also assesses the perceived harmfulness of each abusive event. The reliability coefficient for the Measure of Wife Abuse is approximately .93.

The IA is a 36-item self-report measure of the type, frequency and perceived harmfulness of abuse directed by one intimate partner towards another within a six-month period. The researcher derived this version of the IA by selecting items that loaded most highly onto their respective abuse category.

The IA asks for an estimate of the number of abusive events received over the past six months, or during the last six months, of the most current abusive relationship. In addition, each subject rates how much each event hurt her on a four-point Likert-type scale, ranging from "this never hurt or upset me" (1) to "this often hurt or upset me" (4). The four categories of abuse measured by the IA are: physical (e.g., kicked, pushed, bit), sexual (e.g., raped, forced sex acts, prostituted), psychological (e.g., stole possessions, imprisoned, harassed), and verbal (e.g., told not good, told stupid, called whore). The items contained in the IA are listed in Table 8.

The IA takes approximately 15 minutes to complete, depending on the severity of abuse experienced, and the length of time between the end of the relationship and the time of survey completion (i.e., the longer a woman has been away from the abusive relationship, the more time it takes her to estimate the type and amount of abuse she received). A copy of the IA is contained in Appendix B.

Table 8. Inventory of Abuse Items

Physical abuse items*:
 1. threw objects at you
 2. bit you
 3. punched you
 4. kicked you
 5. hit you with a belt
 6. threw you onto the furniture
 7. shook you
 8. pushed you
 9. whipped you

Sexual abuse items*:
 1. squeezed your breasts
 2. put foreign objects in your vagina
 3. held you down and cut your pubic hair
 4. tried to rape you
 5. raped you
 6. prostituted you
 7. forced you to have sex with other partners
 8. treated you as a sex object
 9. forced you to do unwanted sex acts

Verbal abuse items*:
 1. called you a whore
 2. told you that you were crazy
 3. told you that no one would ever want you
 4. told you that you were lazy
 5. called you a bitch
 6. told you that you were a horrible wife/partner
 7. told you weren't good
 8. told you that you were stupid
 9. told you that you were ugly

Psychological abuse items*:
 1. imprisoned you in your house
 2. harassed you at work
 3. locked you in the bedroom
 4. took your wallet leaving you stranded
 5. stole your possessions
 6. took your car key
 7. disabled your car
 8. harassed you over the telephone
 9. stole food or money from you

*All items begin with "Your partner"

Symptom Measures

The Beck Depression Inventory (BDI)

The 21-item Beck Depression Inventory (BDI; Beck et al., 1961) was used to assess the presence and severity of depressive symptoms. The BDI, is a self-report measure used to assess the patient's subjective experience of depression. The BDI measures the intensity of depression across 21 symptoms of or attitudes related to depression. It generally takes 5–10 minutes to complete, and is scored by summing the ratings given to each item. A higher score indicates a higher level of severity of depression. Beck, Steer, and Garbin (1988), state that a score of less than 10 indicates no or minimal depression; 1- 18 indicates mild to moderate depression; 19-29 indicates moderate to severe depression; and 30–63 indicates severe depression. The BDI split-half reliability is approximately .90, and its test-retest reliability is approximately .75.

The Beck Anxiety Inventory (BAI)

The Beck Anxiety Inventory (BAI; Beck et al., 1988) is a 21-item scale that measures the severity of anxiety in adults and adolescents. The BAI, a self-report measure was used to assess the patient's subjective experience of anxiety. Subjects rate each item, using a 4-point Likert-type scale, from "not at all" (0) to "severely, I could barely stand it" (3). It takes approximately 5–10 minutes to complete, and is scored by summing the ratings given to each item. A higher score indicates a higher level of severity of anxiety. Beck and Steer (1990) recommend that a score of less than 10 be interpreted as normal anxiety; 10–18 indicates mild to moderate anxiety; 19–29 indicates moderate to severe anxiety; and 30–63 indicates severe anxiety. The BAI has an internal consistency reliability of .92, and its test-retest reliability is approximately .73.

The Rosenberg Self Esteem Scale (RSE)

The Rosenberg Self Esteem Scale (RSE; Rosenberg, 1965) is a 10-item self-report measure designed to assess an individual's global feelings of self-worth or self-acceptance. The RSE is scored using a four-point Likert-style response format (strongly agree, agree, disagree, strongly disagree) resulting in a scale range of 0-30, with higher scores representing higher self-esteem. Half of the questions are reverse coded. Rosenberg (1965) suggests that scores between 21–30 indicate high self-esteem; 11–20 indicate moderate self-esteem; and 10 or less be interpreted as low self-esteem. The RSE takes approximately 3–5 minutes to complete, and is scored by summing the ratings given to each item. The internal consistency reliabilities for the measure range from .77 to .88, and the test-retest reliability is approximately .82.

DATA ANALYSIS

Preliminary Analyses

Means, standard deviations and intercorrelations were obtained for all of the variables examined. Descriptions of the demographic characteristics of the participants (e.g., race/ethnicity, SES, abuse status) and summary statistics of the data reported by participants (e.g., reasons for attending the group, number of sessions attended, overall satisfaction, helpfulness ratings, type and harmfulness of abuse, types and levels of self-esteem, depression, and anxiety) were obtained. Pearson *r* correlations were performed to test the relation between variables (e.g., number of sessions attended and length of attendance, type and harmfulness of abuse) to determine whether these variables should be combined in subsequent analyses. Descriptions of the demographic characteristics of the participants are listed in the Subjects section above.

Comparison of Support Group Participants to Crisis Line Callers

A comparison of support group participants to crisis line callers was performed in order to determine the similarities and differences between these groups. T-tests and chi-square analyses were used to compare the demographic characteristics of the support group participants to the sample of abused women calling the Womenspace crisis line. For example, age, race/ethnicity, SES, abuse status and helpfulness ratings for the support groups were compared between groups. In addition, a comparison of crisis line survey respondents to crisis line callers in general was performed to determine the percentage of calls in which callers agreed to complete the survey. Finally, an informal interview of a random sample of crisis line volunteers was also conducted to determine the criteria used by the volunteers to select which callers received/did not receive the survey.

Perceived Efficacy of Services

In order to compare the utilization community and professional services by abused women, a series of Chi-square analyses were performed. In addition, the effectiveness of community and professional services used by abused women, was analyzed via a series of t-tests. A multivariate analysis of variance (MANOVA) was not performed due to the extremely small number of subjects using certain services. The alpha level was adjusted to correct for the multiple t-tests performed. These analyses were performed on the combined sample, and the support group and crisis line samples separately.

Perceived Abuse Harmfulness

A comparison of the perceived harmfulness of physical versus non-physical types of abuse was performed. T-tests were used to compare the subjects' harmfulness ratings of two categories of abuse: physical (including physical and sexual abuse items) and non-physical (including verbal and psychological abuse items) abuse. These analyses were performed only on the support group sample.

Depression, Anxiety and Self-esteem

To investigate the relation between types/severity of abuse and levels of depression, anxiety, and self-esteem among support group participants, exploratory and regression analyses were performed. It was predicted that participants reporting higher levels of overall severity of abuse would also report higher levels of depression and anxiety, and lower levels of self-esteem. A multiple regression analysis was performed to determine the effects of the total level of abuse harmfulness (IA) on total depression (BDI), anxiety (BAI), and self-esteem (RSE) scores. The relation between type of abuse (i.e., the four domains covered in the IA: physical, sexual, psychological, and verbal) and depression (BDI), anxiety (BAI), and self-esteem (RSE) were also computed.

Qualitative Analyses

In addition to the quantitative analyses discussed above, information obtained via open-ended survey questions were analyzed using an inductive process. First, the data was entered into a relational data base (i.e., Paradox). Second, the data was reviewed by the researcher and an independent coder, who identified comment categories. Third, these categories were compared and refined until agreement was reached on each category. Fourth, criteria for coding the comments was established by the researcher. Fifth, the comments were coded by one coder according to the established criteria. Finally, in order to assess reliability, the researcher coded the comments. The inter-rater reliability between the coder and the researcher was .92. The coded comments were analyzed for type of comment, frequency of response type, and the emergent themes within each comment category.

CHAPTER IV

Results

PRELIMINARY ANALYSES

Descriptive Statistics

Support Group Sample

This section contains demographic information, abuse-related variables, depression, anxiety, and self-esteem information, and resource utilization patterns for the support group sample.

The support group participants provided general information such as the number of abusers with whom they had ever been partners, how many children they had, and the number of times they had attempted to leave their most recent abusive relationship. In addition, they provided information on the amount of abuse they had received during the last six months of their most current abusive relationship. The number of abusive events was reported and then grouped by type of abuse (e.g., physical, sexual, psychological, and verbal). The support group participants were also asked to complete the BAI, BDI, and RSE, which were measures of their current levels of anxiety, depression, and self-esteem. Table 9 contains a complete list of the means and standard deviations of these variables for the support group sample.

The majority of women who attended the support groups had been abused by more than one intimate partner during their lives. Leaving their abuser appears to have been difficult for most of the women, taking those who chose to leave an average of 3.5 attempts before successfully ending the relationship. Most of the women had children living at home, and low incomes, which may have influenced their ability to leave the abusive relationship.

Table 9. Support Group Sample: Descriptive Statistics

Variable	N	Mean	SD
No. of Children	65	2.03	1.41
No. of Abusers	66	2.42	3.78
No. of Leave Attempts	63	3.59	4.31
Total No. of Abusive Events (in six month period)	65	496.11	694.46
Physical Abuse Events (# in six month period)	65	73.25	155.26
Sexual Abuse Events (# in six month period)	65	62.00	107.94
Verbal Abuse Events (# in six month period)	65	285.37	398.52
Psychological Abuse Events (# in six month period)	65	75.49	123.22
BAI Score	63	25.65	14.08
BDI Score	65	22.45	10.17
RSE Score	64	16.64	5.78
Total No. of Resources Used	66	5.64	1.63
Living with Abuser	10	(15.2%)	

The support group participants reported experiencing a very high amount of abuse during the last six months of their most current abusive relationship. The average number of abusive events was almost 500. This would mean that these women experienced an average of 2.75 abusive incidents each day. Most of the participants experienced all four types of abuse: physical, sexual, verbal, and psychological.

The most common type of abuse reported was verbal, which consisted of insults and degrading remarks (e.g., called stupid, told not good wife, called whore, etc.). Sixty-three (95.5%) of the support group participants experienced some form of verbal abuse. The subjects received an average of 285 verbally abusive comments over six months, approximately 1.5 per day.

The next most common type of abuse reported was psychological, consisting of controlling, threatening, and intimidating behaviors (e.g., harassed at work, took car keys, imprisoned in house, etc.). Fifty-three (80.3%) of the women experienced some form of psychological abuse. The women received an average of more than 75 psychologically abusive events in six months, with approximately 12.5 incidents per month.

Physical abuse, consisting of physically aggressive acts (e.g., pushing, hitting, punching, etc.) was the third most frequently experienced form of abuse. Fifty (75.8%) support group participants experienced some form of physical abuse. On average, the subjects reported being physically abused more than 73 times in a six-month period. Therefore, these women had been physically assaulted an average of more than 12 times per month.

The least frequent form of abuse reported was sexual (e.g., attempted rape, rape, enforced prostitution, etc.). Forty-five (68.2%) of the women experienced some form of sexual abuse. The participants reported being sexually abused an average of 62 times in six months. This equals an average of approximately 10 sexual assaults per month.

This study revealed that the majority of women attending a support group had clinically significant levels of anxiety and depression. Sixty-three women completed the BAI, with a mean score of 25.65 (*SD* = 14.08). Of those, only 10 women (15.9%) reported normal levels of anxiety (0-9), and 10 participants had scores between 10 and 18, indicating mild levels of anxiety (Beck, Steer, & Garbin, 1988). The majority of the subjects reported moderate to severe levels of anxiety. Nineteen women (30.2%) reported moderate levels of anxiety (19-29), and the 38.1% (n=27) of the women were experiencing severe symptoms of anxiety (30-57) (Beck, et al., 1988).

Similarly, high rates of depression were also present in this sample. Sixty-five women completed the BDI, with a mean score of 22.45 (*SD* = 10.17). Of those, six (9.2%) scored in the non- to minimal range of depression (0-9), and 18 participants (27.7%) reported mild levels of depression (10-18) (Beck & Steer, 1990). Twenty-five subjects (38.5%) had scores between 19 and 29, indicating moderate levels of depression, and 16 (24.6%) experienced severe depressive symptoms (31-44) (Beck & Steer, 1990).

Sixty-four women completed the RSE, with a mean score of 16.64 (*SD* = 5.78). The majority of participants in this study exhibited moderate to high levels of self-esteem. More than 65% of the women (n=42) reported moderate levels of self-esteem (11-20), and 21.9% (n=14), scored in the high range of self-esteem (21-30). Only eight women (12.5%) reported low levels of self-esteem (6-10) (Rosenberg, 1965).

Participants also reported the types of community and professional services that they had ever used for help with domestic violence issues. The participants were asked whether they had ever contacted clergy, counselors, family members, physicians, or police, and whether or not they had ever filed a temporary restraining order (TRO) against their most recent abuser. See Table 10 for the number and percent of support group participants who used each type of resource.

Table 10. Support Group Sample: Resource Utilization

Variable		Frequency	Percent
Ever Contact Regarding Abuse:			
Family			
	Yes	57	86.4
	No	9	13.6
Counselor			
	Yes	54	81.8
	No	12	18.2
Physician			
	Yes	54	81.8
	No	12	18.2
Police			
	Yes	46	69.7
	No	20	30.3
Restraining Order			
	Yes	41	62.1
	No	25	37.9
Lawyer			
	Yes	39	59.1
	No	27	40.9
Clergy			
	Yes	15	22.7
	No	51	77.3

Participants had contacted and/or used many other resources in addition to the support group. These women had used an average of more than five different types of help sources. The most used resources were family, counselors, and physicians. Over 80% of the support group members had discussed their abuse with a primary care physician, and the same percentage had seen a counselor; these two resources were used almost as frequently as family members. This may be due to the severity of the abuse experienced by these women. The large percentage of women contacting the police (69.7%) or filing a restraining order may also support this hypothesis. Over half of the subjects had contacted a lawyer. Only 15 support group participants (22.7%) had ever contacted a member of the clergy regarding their abuse.

The most common reason (44%) women gave for not contacting family members was that they felt it would not help the situation. Eight of the 12 women (67%) who did not contact a physician did not do so because they did not have a primary care physician. Only 12 women had not used the services of a counselor or therapist. The most common reason (25%) cited by those women was the inability to afford counseling. Sixty percent (n=12) of the women who did not contact the police did not do so because they didn't have the need, as was the case for the majority of women who didn't use a lawyer (56%). Of the women who did not contact the clergy, 24 (47%) reported that they did not contact the clergy because they did not belong to a church or synagogue.

Usage of services varied somewhat by the type of abuse that the women experienced. While most resources were used at almost equal rates regardless of type of abuse experienced, police and restraining orders were used more often for physical and psychological abuse than for verbal or sexual abuse. See Table 11 for a complete listing of resource usage by type of abuse.

Table 11. Frequency (%) of Resource Utilization by Type of Abuse Experienced

Resource	Verbal	Psychological	Physical	Sexual
	(n=63)	(n=53)	(n=50)	(n=45)
Clergy	15 (24%)	12 (23%)	11 (22%)	11 (24%)
Counselor	54 (86%)	45 (85%)	42 (84%)	39 (87%)
Family	54 (86%)	46 (87%)	43 (86%)	39 (87%)
Lawyer	38 (60%)	32 (60%)	29 (58%)	26 (58%)
Physician	51 (81%)	44 (77%)	40 (80%)	36 (80%)
Police	44 (70%)	41 (77%)	40 (80%)	33 (73%)
TRO	39 (62%)	36 (68%)	35 (70%)	28 (62%)

Crisis Line Sample

The sections contains only demographic characteristics and resource utilization information for the crisis line sample.

The crisis line callers used an average of more than three types of community and/or professional resources for help with their abuse ($n = 66$, $M = 3.67$, $SD = 1.54$).

Table 12. Crisis Line Sample: Resource Utilization

Variable		Frequency	Percent
Ever Contact Regarding Abuse:			
Family			
	Yes	52	78.8
	No	12	18.2
Counselor			
	Yes	51	77.3
	No	14	21.2
Physician			
	Yes	47	71.2
	No	17	25.8
Police			
	Yes	34	51.5
	No	30	45.5
Clergy			
	Yes	23	34.8
	No	41	62.1
Lawyer			
	Yes	23	34.8
	No	43	65.2
Group			
	Yes	12	18.2
	No	53	80.3

The crisis line subjects also reported the types of community and professional services that they had ever used for help with domestic violence issues. The participants were asked whether they had ever contacted clergy, counselors, family members, physicians, or police, and whether or not they had ever attended a support group for battered women. See Table 12 for the number and percent of crisis line callers who used each type of resource.

Crisis line respondents had different usage rates for the community and professional resources than did the support group members. Overall, crisis line callers used fewer resources than support group members. In addition, all resources except support groups and clergy were used by a smaller percentage of crisis line callers than group members.

The most used resources were the same as for the support group: family, counselors, and physicians. The next most frequently used resource was the police, although the frequency of use was much lower than that of the support group sample.

There were also differences in the use of clergy, lawyers, and support groups by the crisis line sample. Almost 35% of the crisis line callers had contacted a member of the clergy regarding their abuse, and less than 35% of crisis line callers had ever used the services of a lawyer. Finally, only 18% of the crisis line sample had ever attended a battered women's support group.

Combined Sample

The support group and the crisis line samples were combined for these, and subsequent, analyses in order to provide a more representative sample of all abused women. This section contains information of resource utilization for the combined sample.

The two samples were combined to assess the types of community and professional services that they had ever used for help with domestic violence issues. The combined sample used an average of more than four types of community and/or professional resources for help with their abuse ($n = 132$, $M = 4.65$, $SD = 1.87$).

Over 82 percent of the combined sample used family members as a resource for help with domestic violence. The next most frequently used resource was counselors, followed by physicians, the police, support groups, lawyers, and the clergy. See Table 13 for the number and percent of the combined sample who used each type of resource.

Table 13. Combined Sample: Resource Utilization

Variable		Frequency	Percent
Ever Contact Regarding Abuse:			
Family			
	Yes	109	82.6
	No	21	15.9
Counselor			
	Yes	105	79.5
	No	26	19.7
Physician			
	Yes	101	76.5
	No	29	22.0
Police			
	Yes	80	60.6
	No	50	37.9
Group			
	Yes	78	59.1
	No	53	40.2
Lawyer			
	Yes	62	47.0
	No	70	53.0
Clergy			
	Yes	38	28.8
	No	92	69.7

Correlations

Pearson *r* correlations were performed to test the relation between variables and to determine whether these variables should be explored further or combined in subsequent analyses. Correlation analyses were performed separately for the support group and crisis line samples.

Support Group Sample

The relation between variables for the support group sample were obtained via Pearson product moment correlations. Only significant correlations will be described in this section.

There was a strong positive correlation between several demographic variables and measures of anxiety (BAI), depression (BDI), and self-esteem (RSE). Income was the variable most highly correlated with anxiety ($R^2 = -.40$, $p = .001$), depression ($R^2 = -.43$, $p < .001$), and self-esteem ($R^2 = .46$, $p < .001$). The lower the income, the higher the subjects scored on the BAI and BDI, and the lower they scored on the RSE. Age was highly correlated with the BAI, $R^2 = -.30$, $p = .02$, and the BDI, $R^2 = -.29$, $p = .02$. The older the subject, the lower they scored on measures of anxiety and depression. Education was also correlated with the BAI ($R^2 = -.30$, $p = .02$) and the RSE ($R^2 = .34$, $p = .01$). The more educated the subject, the lower their level of anxiety, and the higher they scored on the measure of self-esteem. There was also a significant positive correlation between education and perceived harmfulness of physical abuse, $R^2 = .35$, $p = .01$, suggesting that the more educated a subject, the higher she rated the harmfulness of the physical abuse she experienced.

Several abuse related variables were related to depression and anxiety. In those subjects who were separated from their abusers (n=54), the length of separation was significantly correlated with their level of depression ($R^2 = -.37$, $p < .01$); the longer they were separated, the lower the women scored on the measure of depression. The number of attempts to leave the abusive relationship was positively correlated with level of anxiety ($R^2 = .29$, $p = .03$). The more leave attempts a subject had made, the more likely she was to have higher levels of anxiety. The amount of abuse experienced (IA score) was negatively correlated with self-esteem, $R^2 = -.26$, $p = .04$. The more abuse received, the lower the women scored on the RSE. Of the different types of abuse (e.g., physical, sexual, verbal, psychological), the amount of verbal abuse was negatively correlated with self-esteem, $R^2 = -.33$, $p = .01$.

The number of resources used was related to several variables. Number of resources used was significantly correlated with education ($R^2 = -.26$, $p = .04$), number of children ($R^2 = .30$, $p = .01$), number of leave attempts ($R^2 = .31$, $p = .01$), relationship length ($R^2 = .27$, $p = .03$), and amount of verbal abuse received ($R^2 = .25$, $p = .05$). Women with less education were likely to use more resources; women with more children also used more resources. Subjects who were in relationships for longer and/or had made more attempts to leave the relationship also used more help resources. Number of resources was also positively associated, but not significantly, with age ($R^2 = .23, p = .06$), BAI ($R^2 = .23, p = .07$), IA ($R^2 = .23, p = .06$), and amount of psychological abuse experienced ($R^2 = .24, p = .06$).

The types of resources used were correlated with many demographic and abuse-related variables. The use of clergy was negatively correlated with age ($R^2 = -.31, p = .01$), number of children ($R^2 = -.27, p = .03$), and relationship length ($R^2 = -.43, p < .001$). Seeing a counselor or therapist was negatively correlated with income ($R^2 = -.26, p = .04$). Use of a lawyer was negatively correlated with age ($R^2 = -.23, p = .06$), and relationship length ($R^2 = -.35, p < .01$). Contacting the police was positively correlated with education ($R^2 = .37, p < .01$) and perceived harmfulness of verbal abuse ($R^2 = .26, p = .05$). Use of the police was negatively correlated with anxiety ($R^2 = -.27, p = .03$), depression ($R^2 = -.25, p = .04$), number of leave attempts ($R^2 = -.33, p = .01$), total abuse ($R^2 = -.24, p = .05$), verbal abuse ($R^2 = -.30, p = .02$), and perceived harmfulness of sexual abuse ($R^2 = -.30, p = .04$). Getting a restraining order was negatively correlated with number of children ($R^2 = -.31, p = .01$), and number of leave attempts ($R^2 = -.34, p = .01$).

Many resource helpfulness ratings were correlated with other variables. Whether or not a woman was still living with her abuser was highly correlated with clergy helpfulness ($R^2 = .81, p < .001$). Women who were not living with their abusers were more likely to find the clergy to be helpful. Clergy helpfulness was also related to the amount of sexual abuse ($R^2 = .50, p = .05$) and the perceived harmfulness of sexual abuse ($R^2 = .67, p = .02$). The more sexual abuse and the higher the perceived harmfulness of that abuse, the more helpful the clergy were rated. Support group helpfulness was related to perceived harmfulness of physical abuse ($R^2 = .29, p = .04$), and sexual abuse ($R^2 = .39 p = .01$). The greater the women perceived the harmfulness of the physical and sexual abuse they experienced, the more helpful they rated the group. Lawyer helpfulness was negatively correlated with number of abusers ($R^2 = -.35, p = .03$); the more abusers a women had, the less helpful she rated lawyers to be. Physician helpfulness was related to total perceived abuse harmfulness ($R^2 = .50$, $p < .01$), perceived psychological abuse harmfulness ($R^2 = .43$, $p = .02$), and verbal abuse harmfulness ($R^2 = .44$, $p = .01$). The more harmful the subjects perceived their psychological and verbal abuse, the higher they rated their physicians' helpfulness. Whether or not a woman was still living with her abuser was also correlated with physician helpfulness ($R^2 = .60$, $p < .001$). Women who were not living with their abusers rated their physicians as more helpful. Police helpfulness was also correlated with whether or not a woman was living with her abuser ($R^2 = -.31$, $p = .04$); women who were not living with their abusers rated police as more helpful than those women who were still living with their abusers.

Crisis Line Sample

The relation between variables for the crisis line sample were obtained via Pearson product moment correlations. Only significant correlations will be described in this section.

Education was negatively correlated with length of separation from the abuser ($R^2 = -.34$, $p = .05$); women with lower levels of education were separated from their abusers for longer than were those women with more education. Contacting the clergy was negatively correlated with income ($R^2 = -.24$, $p = .05$). Subjects who contacted the clergy were likely to have less money than those who did not use that resource. Discussing abuse with the family was positively correlated with length of the relationship ($R^2 = .25$, $p = .05$); the longer a woman was in her abusive relationship, the more likely she was to discuss the abuse with family members. Age was correlated with use of a physician ($R^2 = .29$, $p = .02$). Older women were more likely to go to a physician regarding their abuse than were younger women. Income was negatively correlated with use of a support group ($R^2 = -.26$, $p = .04$). Support group participants had lower incomes than those who did not go to a support group. Having insurance was highly correlated with use of a physician ($R^2 = .56$, $p < .001$).

Age was positively correlated with overall group helpfulness ratings ($R^2 = .61$, $p = .04$); older women found the group to be more helpful than did younger women. Having insurance was negatively correlated with overall family helpfulness ratings (R^2 = -.28, p = .05); women with insurance rated family as less helpful than those who did not. Whether or not a woman was still living with her abuser was highly correlated with overall group helpfulness ratings (R^2 = .74, p = .01). Women who were not living with their abusers rated support groups higher than those who were still living with their abusive partners. Length of relationship was negatively correlated with overall clergy helpfulness ratings (R^2 = -.43, p = .04); women who had been in their abusive relationships longer rated the clergy as less helpful.

Comparison of Support Group to Crisis Line Sample

Comparison of Variables

Results of the t-tests and chi-square analyses found no differences between the support group and crisis line samples on most of the study variables. However, the analyses uncovered differences between the support group and crisis line samples on six variables. Three are demographic variables: marital status, living with abuser status, and employment status. The other three variables are related to utilization of the following services: support groups, lawyers, and police.

Support group participants were more likely to be single than crisis line callers (c^2 = -2.80, p = .005). Figure 1 illustrates this difference in marital status. Support group participants were also much less likely to be living with their abuser (c^2 = -3.46, p = .0005). Figure 2 illustrates the difference in living with abuser status. Support group participants were more likely to be employed, either full- or part-time, and less likely to be students or unemployed than the crisis line callers (c^2 = -2.60, p = .009). Figure 3 illustrates the differences between the samples in employment status.

Because data was collected from a support group sample, there was, by definition, a difference between samples on support group attendance. There was 100% attendance in the support group sample versus only 18% in the crisis line sample (c^2 = -9.42, p = .0000). There were other differences between samples in the utilization of resources. The support group participants were more likely to use the services of a lawyer (c^2 = -2.89, p = .004), and were more likely to contact the police ($c^2 = -2.01$, p = .04) than were the crisis line callers. Figures 4 and 5 illustrate these differences between the samples.

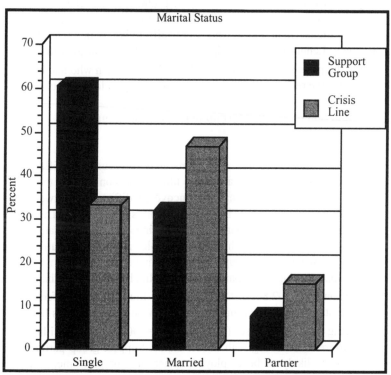

Figure 1. Differences in Marital Status between Samples

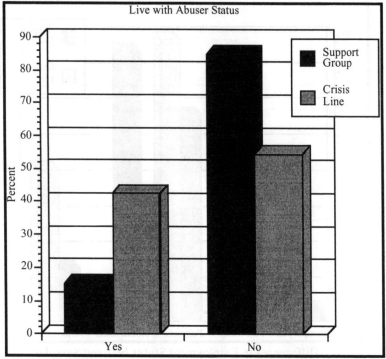

Figure 2. Differences in Living with Abuser Status between Samples

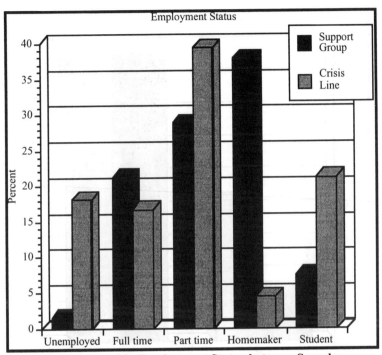

Figure 3. Differences in Employment Status between Samples

Helping Survivors of Domestic Violence

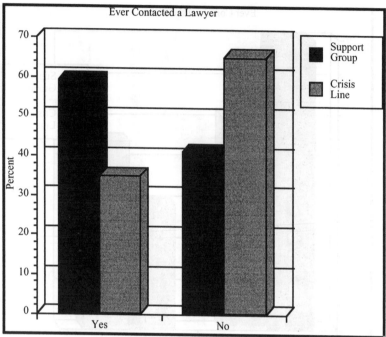

Figure 4. Differences in Use of Lawyer between Samples

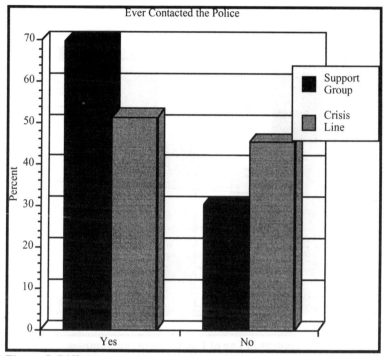

Figure 5. **Differences in Use of Police between Samples**

PERCEIVED EFFICACY OF SERVICES

The support group participants and crisis line callers rated the helpfulness of each type of community/professional resource that they had ever used on a scale of 1 (not at all helpful) to 4 (very helpful). In addition, the support group participants indicated how helpful specific factors (e.g., providing information, giving support, etc.) were for each type of service. Due to the significant differences between the samples in utilization of services, and the additional variables present in the support group data, analyses on perceived effectiveness of services were done separately for each sample.

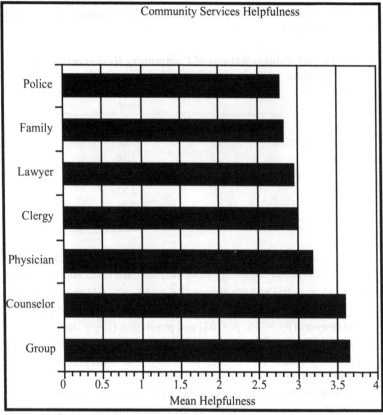

Figure 6. Resource Helpfulness Ratings: Support Group Sample

Support Group Sample

Overall, these subjects rated support groups and counselors as the most helpful resources, and family and police as the least helpful. Resource helpfulness ratings are presented in Figure 6. Support groups, counselors, and physicians were rated as somewhat helpful to very helpful. Members of the clergy were rated as somewhat helpful. Lawyers, family members, and the police were rated as neither helpful/nor unhelpful to somewhat helpful. Support groups and counselors received consistently high ratings, while other resources received more varied ratings. Means and standard deviations for support group subjects' helpfulness ratings of community resources are listed in Table 14.

Table 14. Helpfulness Ratings of Community Resources: Support Group Sample

Resource	N	Mean	SD
Group	66	3.65	.48
Counselor/Therapist	53	3.60	.53
Physician	38	3.18	.98
Clergy	15	3.00	1.00
Lawyer	39	2.95	1.12
Family	57	2.83	1.01
Police	45	2.78	1.15

A variety of resources were used and rated by the participants. Women who found the clergy to be helpful, also rated support groups ($R^2 = .52$, $p = .05$) and physicians ($R^2 = .63$, $p = .04$) to be helpful in dealing with their abuse. Subjects who rated family as helpful, also found lawyers ($R^2 = .36$, $p = .03$) and physicians ($R^2 = .46$, $p = .01$) to be helpful. The helpfulness of group was also positively correlated with lawyer helpfulness ($R^2 = .32$, $p = .05$). The correlations between helpfulness ratings are presented in Table 15.

T-tests were used to compare the helpfulness of support groups to that of other resources. Results of the t-test indicated that the support groups were rated significantly more helpful than physicians ($t = 2.49$, df = 37, $p = .02$), clergy ($t = -3.59$, df = 14, $p = .003$), lawyers ($t = 4.34$, df = 38, $p < .001$), family ($t = -6.04$, df = 56, $p < .001$), and police ($t = 4.85$, df = 44, $p < .001$). There were no differences between support group and counselor helpfulness ratings ($t = -.22$, df = 52, $p = .83$).

The support group participants also rated specific components of the group that they found to be helpful. The subjects were asked to rate the helpfulness of eight components of the group. Table 16 contains a complete list of group components and their helpfulness rating means and standard deviations.

Table 15. Correlations between Helpfulness Ratings for Community Resources: Support Group Sample

	Clergy	Counsel	Family	Group	Lawyer	Physician	Police
Clergy	1.00						
	(15)						
	—						
Counsel	.26	1.00					
	(13)	(53)					
	p=.39	—					
Family	.47	-.19	1.00				
	(14)	(48)	(57)				
	p=.09	p=.19	—				
Group	.52	.23	.18	1.00			
	(15)	(53)	(57)	(66)			
	p=.05	p=.10	p=.18	—			
Lawyer	.42	-.10	.36	.32	1.00		
	(14)	(34)	(36)	(39)	(39)		
	p=-.14	p=.59	p=.03	p=.05	—		
Physician	.63	-.25	-.46	-.02	.15	1.00	
	(11)	(30)	(33)	(38)	(26)	(38)	
	p=.04	p=.18	p=.01	p=.89	p=.45	—	
Police	.16	-.19	.03	.03	.27	-.32	1.00
	(11)	(36)	(40)	(45)	(28)	(27)	(45)
	p=.63	p=.26	p=.85	p=.86	p=.16	p=.10	—

Table 16. Helpfulness Ratings of Support Group Components

Component	N	Mean	SD
Hearing from others	66	3.94	.30
Safe place to talk	65	3.78	.65
Support from others	65	3.77	.46
Information about abuse	66	3.70	.55
Discussions/exercises	57	3.63	.67
Making friends	66	3.20	.83
Time away from home	62	3.13	.95
Free child care	38	2.89	1.52

Seven components of the groups were found to be somewhat helpful to very helpful. Participants rated "hearing from others in the same situation" as the most helpful aspect of the group ($M = 3.94$), followed by "having a safe place to talk" ($M = 3.78$), "receiving support from other group members and/or facilitators" ($M = 3.77$), "receiving information about domestic violence" ($M = 3.70$), "participating in discussions or group exercises" ($M = 3.63$), "meeting other women who might become friends" ($M = 3.20$), and "having time away from home for myself" ($M = 3.13$). Component helpfulness ratings are presented in Figure 7.

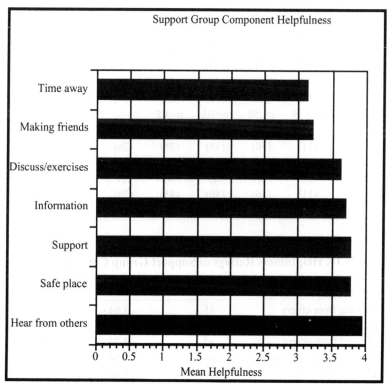

Figure 7. Support Group Component Helpfulness Ratings

The support group participants also rated specific components of the other community/professional services that they used. The subjects were asked to rate the helpfulness of four components: 1) letting you know that you are not alone in your situation; 2) providing a safe place to talk; 3) providing support and encouragement; 4) providing information and/or referrals on domestic violence/abuse. Table 17 contains a complete list of service components and their helpfulness rating means and standard deviations.

Table 17. Helpfulness Ratings of Professional/Community Service Components

Component	N	Mean	SD
Counselors			
Providing a safe place to talk	54	3.89	.37
Letting you know you are not alone	54	3.78	.50
Providing support and encouragement	54	3.76	.47
Providing information & referral	54	3.48	.79
Clergy			
Providing support and encouragement	15	2.93	1.22
Providing a safe place to talk	15	2.87	1.19
Letting you know you are not alone	15	2.80	1.37
Providing information & referral	15	2.33	1.29
Lawyers			
Providing a safe place to talk	39	3.23	.87
Providing support and encouragement	38	2.84	1.05
Letting you know you are not alone	37	2.78	1.03
Providing information & referral	37	2.51	1.17
Physicians			
Providing a safe place to talk	37	3.14	1.08
Providing support and encouragement	37	3.03	1.19
Letting you know you are not alone	37	2.84	1.12
Providing information & referral	37	2.54	.96
Police			
Providing a safe place to talk	45	2.71	1.16
Providing support and encouragement	45	2.40	1.18
Providing information & referral	45	2.38	1.15
Letting you know you are not alone	45	2.38	1.13

Similar components were found to be somewhat to very helpful when using counselors, lawyers, family, and physicians. Subjects found counselors (M = 3.89), lawyers (M = 3.23), family (M = 3.14), and physicians (M = 3.14) somewhat to very helpful in "providing a safe place to talk." They also reported that counselors were somewhat to very helpful in "letting [them] know they were not alone in their situation" (M = 3.78), and "providing information and referrals on domestic violence" (M = 3.48). Counselors (M = 3.76), family (M = 3.05), and physicians (M = 3.03) were all found to be somewhat to very helpful in "providing support and encouragement." Component helpfulness ratings for these services are presented in Figure 8.

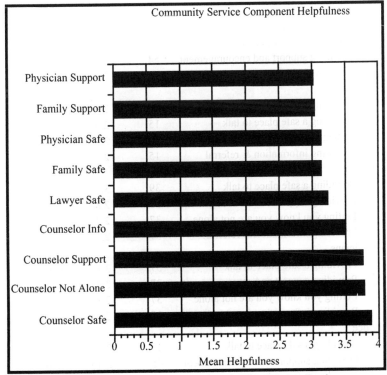

Figure 8. Community Service Component Helpfulness Ratings

Crisis Line Sample

Overall, the crisis line subjects rated support groups and counselors as the most helpful resources, and clergy and police as the least helpful. Resource helpfulness ratings are presented in Figure 9. Support groups, counselors, and physicians were rated as somewhat helpful to very helpful. Family, lawyers, members of the clergy, and the police were rated as neither helpful/nor unhelpful to somewhat helpful. There appeared to be more variability in the helpfulness ratings for this sample than for the support group sample. Means and standard deviations for support group subjects' helpfulness ratings of community resources are listed in Table 18.

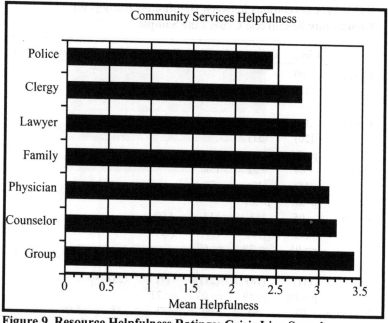

Figure 9. Resource Helpfulness Ratings: Crisis Line Sample

Table 18. Helpfulness Ratings of Community Resources: Crisis Line Sample

Resource	N	Mean	SD
Group	12	3.42	.67
Counselor/Therapist	51	3.20	1.00
Physician	30	3.10	1.30
Family	52	2.90	1.21
Lawyer	23	2.83	1.23
Clergy	23	2.78	1.17
Police	32	2.44	1.22

Table 19. Correlations between Helpfulness Ratings for Community Resources: Crisis Line Sample

	Clergy	Counsel	Family	Group	Lawyer	Physician	Police
Clergy	1.00						
	(23)						
	—						
Counsel	.08	1.00					
	(20)	(51)					
	p=.74	—					
Family	-.04	-.02	1.00				
	(18)	(40)	(52)				
	p=.87	p=.89	—				
Group	-.05	.13	.14	1.00			
	(9)	(12)	(11)	(12)			
	p=.91	p=.70	p=.69	—			
Lawyer	.56	.14	.48	.17	1.00		
	(11)	(18)	(21)	(7)	(23)		
	p=-.08	p=.59	p=.03	p=.72	—		
Physician	.03	.50	.00	.72	.38	1.00	
	(15)	(23)	(25)	(9)	(15)	(30)	
	p=.91	p=.02	p=.99	p=.03	p=.17	—	
Police	-.34	-.09	.20	.07	-.22	.12	1.00
	(17)	(26)	(27)	(7)	(16)	(15)	(32)
	p=.19	p=.65	p=.32	p=.88	p=.40	p=.67	—

A variety of resources were used and rated by the crisis line callers. Women who found counselors to be helpful, also rated physicians (R^2 = .50, p = .02) to be helpful in dealing with their abuse. Subjects who rated family as helpful, also found lawyers (R^2 = .48, p = .03) to be helpful. The helpfulness of group was also positively correlated with physician helpfulness (R^2 = .72, p = .03). The correlations between helpfulness ratings are presented in Table 19.

T-tests comparing support groups to other resources could not be performed due to the extremely small number of crisis line callers who had used the services of a support group (n = 12).

Combined Sample

The support group and crisis line samples were combined in order to perform resource helpfulness comparisons on a more representative sample of abused women.

Overall, subjects in the combined sample rated support groups and counselors as the most helpful resources, and family and police as the least helpful. Resource helpfulness ratings are presented in Figure 10. Support groups, counselors, and physicians were rated as somewhat helpful to very helpful. Lawyers, members of the clergy, family members, and the police were rated as neither helpful/nor unhelpful to somewhat helpful. Means and standard deviations for support group subjects' helpfulness ratings of community resources are listed in Table 20.

Table 20. Helpfulness Ratings of Community Resources: Combined Sample

Resource	N	Mean	SD
Group	78	3.62	.52
Counselor/Therapist	104	3.40	.82
Physician	68	3.15	1.12
Lawyer	62	2.90	1.16
Clergy	38	2.87	1.09
Family	109	2.87	1.11
Police	77	2.64	1.18

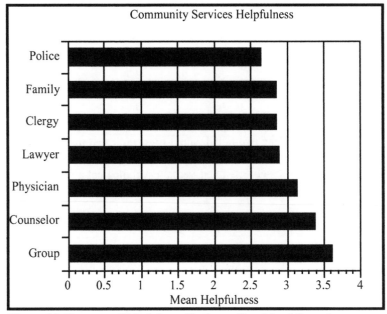

Figure 10. Resource Helpfulness Ratings: Combined Sample

The results of the t-tests comparing support groups to other resources were similar to those of the support group sample. Support groups were rated significantly more helpful than physicians (t = 2.44, df = 46, p = .02), clergy (t = -2.51, df = 23, p = .02), lawyers (t = 4.38, df = 45, p < .001), family (t = -5.82, df = 67, p < .001), and police (t = 5.18, df = 51, p < .001). There were no differences between support group and counselor helpfulness ratings (t = -.17, df = 64, p = .87).

ABUSE HARMFULNESS RATINGS

In addition to the amount and type of abuse experienced, the support group participants also reported how much each type of abuse hurt or upset them. Overall, the women in this sample rated all types of abuse as very hurtful or upsetting. Means and standard deviations for abuse harmfulness ratings are contained in Table 21.

Table 21. Harmfulness Ratings by Type of Abuse

Type of Abuse	N	Mean	SD
Psychological	53	3.81	.32
Physical	50	3.78	.39
Verbal	63	3.77	.31
Sexual	46	3.67	.57

The results of the two-tailed paired t-test indicated that there were no differences for perceived harmfulness of physical versus non-physical abuse; the subjects rated verbal/psychological abuse to be as harmful as physical/sexual assault (see Table 22).

Table 22. Comparison of Perceived Harmfulness of Abuse

	Physical/Sexual Mean (SD) (n=55)	Verbal/Psychological Mean (SD) (n=55)	p
Perceived Harmfulness	3.75 (.34)	3.79 (.28)	.38

PSYCHOSOCIAL CORRELATES OF ABUSE

It was predicted that participants reporting higher levels of overall severity of abuse would also report higher levels of depression and anxiety, and lower levels of self-esteem. Multiple regression analyses were performed to determine the effects of the total amount of abuse (IA) on total depression (BDI), anxiety (BAI), and self-esteem (RSE) scores. The multiple regression analyses failed to show significant effects on the amount of abuse (IA score) as a predictor of level of depression (BDI) or anxiety (BAI). These results indicate that total amount of abuse does not provide predictive information on the level of depression and anxiety in abused women. Follow-up analyses were not warranted.

The multiple regression analysis approached significance on the measure of self-esteem (RSE), $F (2, 60) = 10.47, p =.054$, adjusted $R^2 = .23$, suggesting that the total amount of abuse experienced (IA score) may be indicative of differences in how abused women perceive themselves in response to repeated abuse.

In addition, it was hypothesized that depression, anxiety, and self-esteem would change as a function of whether or not a woman was still in her abusive relationship, multiple regression analyses were performed on a split sample: those subjects who were still living with their abusers versus those who were separated. The multiple regression analyses failed to show significant effects on the amount of abuse (IA) as a predictor of level of depression (BDI) or self-esteem (RSE) in either group (i.e., live with abuser, don't live with abuser). However, a trend was found on the IA as a predictor of level of anxiety (BAI), F (2,7) = 11.35, p = .08, adjusted R^2 = .70 for the small sample of women still living with their abuser (n=9).

For those women who were no longer living with their abuser, length of separation was thought to be associated with levels of depression, anxiety, and self-esteem. Multiple regression analyses were performed to determine the effect of separation length (seplong) on depression (BDI), anxiety (BAI), and self-esteem (RSE). The omnibus F-test was significant for separation length as a predictor of level of depression, F (1, 52) = 8.42, p = .005, adjusted R^2 = .12. The analyses failed to show significant effects on separation length as a predictor of level of anxiety or self-esteem.

Pearson product moment correlations were performed to examine the relation between type of abuse and depression, anxiety, and self-esteem. The correlations between type of abuse (i.e., the four domains covered in the IA: physical, sexual, verbal, and psychological) and depression (BDI), anxiety (BAI), and self-esteem (RSE) are listed in Table 23.

A significant negative correlation was found between amount of verbal abuse and level of self-esteem (RSE), R^2 = -.33, p <.01; the greater the amount of verbal abuse, the lower the RSE. A trend towards a negative correlation was found between the amount of physical abuse and the level of self-esteem (R^2 = -.23, p =.07). A trend towards a positive correlation was found between the amount of verbal abuse and the level of anxiety (R^2 = .21, p =.09). This analysis did not reveal any other significant correlations between the abuse and psychosocial variables.

Table 23. Correlations between Type of Abuse and BAI, BDI, and RSE

	BAI	BDI	RSE	Phys	Sexual	Verbal	Psych
BAI	1.00						
	(63)						
	—						
BDI	.69	1.00					
	(63)	(65)					
	p<.00	—					
RSE	-.59	-.66	1.00				
	(63)	(64)	(64)				
	p<.00	p<.00	—				
Phys	.17	.08	-.23	1.00			
	(63)	(65)	(64)	(65)			
	p=.19	p=.52	p=.07	—			
Sexual	-.03	-.15	.04	.74	1.00		
	(63)	(65)	(64)	(65)	(65)		
	p=-.83	p=.24	p=.74	p=.00	—		
Verbal	.21	.17	-.33	.67	.54	1.00	
	(63)	(65)	(64)	(65)	(65)	(65)	
	p=.09	p=.18	p<.01	p<.01	p<.01	—	
Psych	.16	.04	-.16	.77	.65	.19	1.00
	(63)	(65)	(64)	(65)	(65)	(65)	(65)
	p=.22	p=.73	p=.22	p<.01	p<.01	p<.01	—

QUALITATIVE ANALYSES

Content analyses were conducted on the comments contained in the support group survey. Sixty-four subjects (97%) wrote at least one comment regarding the support group. A total of 202 comments were analyzed for content and coded. The comments were grouped into one of five major categories: 1) reasons for attending group (11% of total comments); 2) helpful components of group (44%); 3) not helpful parts of the group (4%); 4) suggestions for improvement (33%); and 5) miscellaneous responses (8%).

Reasons for Attending Group

This category contained 22 comments. These comments expressed a variety of reasons that the subjects reported for initially attending a support group, or for continuing to participate in the groups. Five themes, or sub-categories, emerged from these comments. The first theme, expressing the most common reason for attending the support group, was to talk to and/or hear from others in the same situation. The next most common reason for attending the group was to learn more about domestic abuse. The third sub-category of reasons had to do with new facilitators coming to learn about the support groups. Being ordered or asked to attend the group by others, and miscellaneous reasons for attending were the fourth and fifth themes that emerged from within this category. The following comments are representative of those contained in this category:

"I need to be heard and listened to, don't [sic] to be told it's all my fault."

"Different reasons as I go through different stages. At first, I was trying to learn how to deal with the abuse: now I want to get strong and stay away from abusive people."

"Because I know I need help to get through this to be strong and to never do this again (getting in another abusive relationship).

Helpful Components of the Group

The majority of comments (88) fell into this category. Participants identified many aspects of the support group that they found helpful. Three major themes emerged from the comments in this category. Talking to and hearing from others in the same situation was the part of the group most commonly cited as being helpful. The majority of comments in this category elaborated on this theme. Ending isolation, learning that they were not crazy, and the support and encouragement received from other group members were commonly mentioned items. The second most common theme was the helpfulness of information on abuse and community resources. Many subjects reported that the information they learned about abuse was very useful for helping them recognize abuse, getting out of abusive relationships, and staying away from their abusers. The third sub-category contained comments that were general in nature. These comments gave general praise to the facilitators of the groups and to the domestic violence agency sponsoring the support group programs. Examples of comments that comprise this category follow:

"I need to talk to people who can validate my experience and can understand what I went through. When I heard the other women and the counselor speak I felt less crazy and realized it was good I got out since I wasn't able to make my husband recognized what was wrong."

"It's very helpful to be around other women who know what you're talking about. And also to hear that what they're saying sounds very familiar. The facilitators have given me the feeling that I was listened to, heard, encouraged. They have given me valuable information about community resources."

"Talking about my situation, discussing it with someone who knows the cycle of abuse and letting me know that it is normal to feel alone and afraid."

"Group has been great. Facilitators very caring—always prepared. I learned a lot about myself and about how others share my story. It feels good to have a place to talk & listen with people who have been through trauma & abuse."

"I have never been in a support group before. So therefor [sic] I didn't know what to expect. I found respect and understanding and that's what I was hoping for."

"The information from the facilitator—on local help group—was good . . . Seeing myself in others. Learning what is emotional abuse . . . Having a place to express my fears, frustrations and hopes. Seeing my progress weekly."

"Because I can feel safe, and understood and I don't have people telling me what to do. If I thought about going back to my husband it would help a lot because I would remember the pain."

Not Helpful Parts of the Group

There were only 8 comments in this category. All of these comments were about one of two issues: child care and making friends. The women who wrote these comments indicated that they either found the child care to be lacking, or they did not need/use these services. They also indicated that making friends was not a priority for them, nor was it something that they had hoped to get from attending the support group.

"Years ago I went to an evening group. The women took turns watching the kids. the kids ran in and out of the group and were worse than distracting. I was ready to hit somebody myself by the end of the group."

"I needed information—not friends—though I have made some here. And I didn't need child care."

"The items that I put not helpful [child care, meeting others who might become friends] were things that I was not needing."

Suggestions for Improvement

This category contained 67 comments, making it the second largest category. The participants made many excellent suggestions for enhancing the groups, and changing procedures that they felt were not working well. There were four emergent themes from these comments. The most common suggestions were to add more information about other community resources (e.g., legal, mental health, etc.), and more exercises (e.g., skills training, recognizing abuse, building self-esteem, etc.). The second largest sub-category of comments were regarding better facilitation of the group process (e.g., limit "storytelling," insure that everyone gets time to speak). The third theme contained in this category was overall satisfaction, or lack of suggestions for improvement. Several women commented that they would not change anything in the group. The final sub-category consisted of miscellaneous suggestions for improvement that did not fit into any of the above themes (e.g., "having some coffee or tea would be a nice thing . . . "). Examples of common themes are listed below:

"Videos of not acceptable behaviors of abusers; or a list of put downs; magazine articles; books on abuse, etc."

"List of police officers in the Eugene/Springfield area who have participated in domestic violence awareness training programs. Names of lawyers in these towns who are women's rights advocates. Names of women who will provide safe homes for women who might not be able to go to shelters, telephone numbers of counselors, support group contacts, 12-step programs, etc. Lists of property managers in town."

"Describing what abuse is and how to recognize it in other people, tools, to identify it in a person you maybe interested in and not getting involved."

"I would like maybe some sort of program that educates women on all forms of abuse so we can recognize it . . . "

"I would like to see more "positive" things added. Such as hair styling, make-up, exercise, community service, job search information, how to dress for job interviews, job networking. Perhaps a video on survival techniques for the battered women, and how to deal with police and district attorneys office."

"I would appreciate more facilitation perhaps a talking stick or a timer . . . to keep some people from monopolizing the group. "

"Facilitators should not allow excessive story telling by any member of the group. More focus on feelings and building skills to cope . . . "

"The support group is just what I need. I wouldn't do anything differently. It's just perfect the way it is."

MISCELLANEOUS

The remaining 17 comments fell into this category. These comments covered a wide range of topics related to abuse, the participant's current situation, and/or general thoughts and feelings that had nothing to do with the support group per se.

"I really love my partner (ex). I feel he has changed. And I'd like us to get back together."

"I would like to know if you need volunteers for women space. Shelters, if there is an y way I can help, mothers and children, all women in the shelters."

"I am learning a new way of living. My husband was a different kind of abuser than this man and I have learned greatly from the combination of the two relationships. I am learning to take care of myself, I am involved in this support group, AA and turning points. I'm setting goals and I'm realizing I am a worthwhile person who deserves respect. There are days that are hard but they keep getting farther apart. If I could help you further in anyway you could give me a call. I feel somehow driven to help in the fight to do what I can to stop domestic violence. I plan to go to CARDVA [domestic violence agency] training in December and start my own group here in Albany. Then by next fall start classes to get a two year degree in counseling. I'm glad to see your interest in Domestic Violence and I'll help if I can."

These comments reflect the thoughts and feelings of a wide range of support group participants (e.g., newcomers and those who had been attending for many years). The participants spent several minutes thinking about and writing their comments, and reported that they were pleased and "honored" to be asked for their opinions regarding the support groups. Several women expressed interest in participating in future research studies.

CHAPTER V

Discussion

SUMMARY OF FINDINGS

This study was designed to systematically assess the efficacy of community, medical, and mental health services for abused women, and the impact of abuse on those women. Specifically, support group participants and crisis line callers were asked about their usage and the perceived helpfulness of support groups, counselors/therapists, physicians, lawyers, clergy, police, and family members. This study found that family, counselors, and physicians were the most widely used resources, and clergy was the least used. Family, the most used resource, was rated as one of the least helpful. Support groups, which were used less frequently than most of the other services, were rated as the most helpful resource.

Support group participants were also asked to identify specifically what they found to be helpful about the services that they used. The participants rated hearing from others in the same situation as the most helpful component of the support groups, followed by having a safe place to talk, receiving support from others, getting information about abuse and local resources, and participating in group discussions and exercises. Providing a safe place to talk was rated as the most helpful part of going to a counselor, lawyer, physician, and the police. Subjects also reported that support and encouragement was the most helpful thing provided by the clergy.

A comparison of support group participants and crisis line callers was conducted to assess for differences in demographic characteristics, service utilization and perceived effectiveness. Crisis line callers were much more likely to still be married and living with their abuser than were the support group participants. Crisis line callers were also less likely to be employed than were support group participants. Crisis line callers used fewer resources than did the support group members; specifically, they were less likely to have used the services of the police and lawyers, and were much less likely to have attended a support group.

Information about the type and severity of abuse experienced by support group participants was also collected during this study. The type and frequency of abuse were assessed, as well as the subjects' perceived harmfulness ratings of that abuse. The support group participants reported receiving high amounts of abuse during the last six months of their most recent abusive relationship. Almost all of these women experienced all four types of abuse: physical, sexual, verbal, and psychological. Most of the subjects were verbally abused every day during the six month period. Over three quarters of the participants experienced psychological and physical abuse at least several times per month. More than half of the respondents were sexually abused on a monthly basis during the last six months of their abusive relationship. All forms of abuse were rated as very hurtful or upsetting. There were no differences in the ratings of perceived harmfulness of physical (physical and sexual) versus non-physical (verbal and psychological) types of abuse. The women who participated in this study reported non-physical abuse to be as harmful as physical and sexual assault.

This study also explored the relation between domestic abuse and the levels of depression, anxiety, and self-esteem among participants of the support groups. It was predicted that participants reporting higher levels of abuse would also report higher levels of depression and anxiety, and lower levels of self-esteem. Results of this study failed to show that the total amount of abuse was predictive of levels of depression and anxiety. However, the findings suggest that the amount of abuse experienced may indicate the victim's level of self-esteem. A significant negative correlation was found between the amount of verbal abuse and level of self-esteem. For those women who were no longer living with their abuser, length of separation was a significant predictor of level of depression.

PERCEIVED HARMFULNESS OF ABUSE

One of the most interesting findings from this study is the perceived harmfulness of the non-physical abuse experienced by the participants. While this and previous community studies (Gelles & Straus, 1988; Gelles & Cornell, 1990) have found non-physical abuse to be much more common than physical or sexual violence, most research on the consequences of abuse does not include assessment specifically for non-physical abuse. Neither does this research attempt to determine the differential effects of those two types of abuse, and no previous research has explored the perceived harmfulness of physical versus non-physical forms of abuse.

Based on the prevalence of verbal and psychological abuse, the levels of psychological and somatic problems associated with domestic violence, and anecdotal information obtained from support group participants, it was anticipated that these women would rate non-physical abuse to be as harmful as, or more harmful than, physical abuse. This hypothesis was supported by the two-tailed paired t-test, which found no differences for perceived harmfulness of physical versus non-physical abuse; the subjects rated verbal/psychological abuse to be as harmful as physical/sexual assault.

Except for a few community studies on prevalence of abuse, almost all research on domestic violence is concerned with physical forms of abuse. Only one outcome study reviewed was specifically aimed at survivors of psychological and/or verbal abuse. Primarily this is due to the difficulty in measuring verbal and psychological abuse. Most researchers believe that measurement of physical abuse is more objective and quantifiable than non-physical abuse. The standard measures for domestic violence (e.g., the Conflict Tactics Scale, Straus 1979) assess for physical aggression and coercive behaviors, but do not address less overt acts.

However, this study, and community prevalence studies, indicate that non-physical abuse is more common than physical abuse. In addition, verbal and psychological abuse tend to precede physical assault in most abusive relationships. The results of this study suggest that verbal and psychological abuse may have consequences similar to physical forms of violence. These consequences might be psychological and/or somatic in nature. Non-physical abuse may have serious mental health consequences, such as heightened depression and anxiety, and lowered self-esteem. In addition, somatic complaints, such as chronic fatigue and headaches, which have been linked to domestic abuse, may be a result of verbal or psychological, rather than physical or sexual abuse. Therefore, the identification of non-physical abuse can be crucial to helping its victims.

UTILIZATION AND PERCEIVED EFFICACY OF SERVICES

The results of this study both contradicted and confirmed previous findings on resource utilization by battered women. Contrary to previous research on resource utilization (Bowker & Maurer, 1986; Horton et al., 1988), this study found that very few women contacted the clergy. In addition, the results of this study showed that many more women used the services of counselors/therapists or physicians than have previous studies (Bowker & Maurer, 1986).

The participants in this study indicated that they did not use the services of the clergy primarily because they did not belong to a church or synagogue. This finding does not conform to national trends, which indicate that more people are attending church on a regular basis than they did ten years ago (Ploch & Hastings, 1995). Many of the subjects were separated or divorced, and perhaps they were more transient or new to this geographic area, and had not time to become involved with a local religious organization. Unfortunately, length of time living in this area was not assessed, therefore this hypothesis must remain conjecture. It is also possible that these women had poor experiences with clergy members (based on the low overall helpfulness ratings of those women still attending church) and had left their church.

The high usage of counselors and therapists may be due to several factors. First, the recognition that domestic violence is a widespread problem may have de-stigmatized battered women. These women may then feel more comfortable discussing their abuse with those professionals whom they believe are trained to help them with the problem. Second, this geographic area has a large number of counselors and therapists, and several low-cost mental health services, making access to counseling relatively easy. Third, most of the subjects in this study had some form of health insurance, which may cover limited psychological services. Finally, half of the sample had been attending a support group, most of which are co-facilitated by counselors or therapists, who advocate the use of mental health specialists to survivors of domestic abuse.

Many more participants in this study used the services of a physician than was anticipated. The high levels of abuse experienced by the subjects, and the resultant physical and mental health consequences, may explain, in part, the high proportion of women who had contacted a physician about their abuse. In addition, most of the subjects in this study had health insurance (which facilitates the use of physicians), and this may help to explain this finding.

Only 18% of the crisis line sample had ever attended a battered women's support group, which confirms previous research that indicates support groups to be one of the least used resources for abused women (Bowker, 1988; Bowker & Maurer, 1986; Donato & Bowker, 1984). There are many factors that contribute to the low usage of support groups. First, and foremost, is the lack of availability of support groups. The geographic area in which this study was conducted contained four domestic violence agencies. These agencies offered from one to three community support groups per week. While the larger communities offered groups on more than one day and time per week, the smaller towns could provide only one group per week. This limited group schedule may be an obstacle for many women. In addition, groups are generally offered only in cities or towns, and women living in more rural areas do not have access.

Second, most domestic violence agencies neither have the funds for, nor want to disclose the locations of support groups via, advertising. Therefore, many abused women never learn of the services provided by their local domestic violence agency—especially the groups. Unless abused women call a crisis line, and telephone counselors tell them about the groups, it is unlikely that they would ever know about the existence of community support groups.

Finally, for many abused women, embarrassment keeps them from attending groups. Especially in smaller cities and towns, it is difficult to remain anonymous in a drop-in community support group. Many battered women report that their abusers are prominent members of the community, and they would not feel comfortable disclosing their problems in public. In addition, humiliation and self-blame keep many abused women from attending support groups, because they believe they are somehow responsible for being in their abusive situation.

The results of this study indicate that the most used resources are not necessarily the most helpful. Both support group participants and crisis line callers rated family members and police, two of the most frequently used resources, as the least helpful for assisting them with domestic violence. The subjects reported that family members were somewhat helpful in providing a safe place to talk and being supportive, but not helpful in letting them know that they are not alone (in being abused), and providing information about domestic violence. While it could be argued that family members should be expected to provide just support and encouragement, and not information about domestic violence, it is that information and the knowledge that they are not alone that abused women report as being especially helpful.

The participants in this study rated police as not helpful in assisting them with domestic violence. They reported that the police did not provide a safe place to talk, information on domestic violence, or support. While it is not the role of the police to provide support and encouragement to victims of domestic violence, police should be creating a safe environment in which victims of violence can at least describe their abuse. In addition, despite recent attempts to train police officers to refer abused women to domestic violence agencies, it appears that law enforcement officials still are not sufficiently aware of local resources, or are reluctant to distribute the information on a regular basis.

In summary, the three most helpful resources identified by study subjects were support groups, counselors/therapists, and physicians. Support groups, as described above, were one of the least used resources. However, both support group participants and crisis line callers rated the groups as very helpful in providing support, information, a safe place to talk, and letting them know they were not alone. The support group participants identified (via objective and open-ended questions) the information about domestic violence, and the ability to talk to and hear from others in the same situation as being extremely important in helping them deal with their abuse. Counselors and therapists were rated as highly as the support groups on the same dimensions of helpfulness (i.e., information, support, safe place, and letting them know they are not alone).

A somewhat startling finding was that physicians were rated as somewhat to very helpful in aiding women with their abuse—almost as highly as counselors and therapists. Subjects found physicians to be helpful in providing a safe place to talk, and being supportive and encouraging. Physicians were rated as somewhat helpful in letting abused women know they weren't alone, and in providing information or referrals about domestic violence. The results of this study indicate that physicians are perceived of as helpful when abused women ask for assistance with domestic violence issues.

DIFFERENCES BETWEEN SAMPLES

The differences between the crisis line and support group samples indicate that women who call the crisis line may be at a different stage in seeking help with their abuse. Crisis line callers were more likely to be married and still living with their abuser than were the support group participants. In addition, the crisis line callers were less likely to be employed, and used fewer community and professional resources (specifically support groups, lawyers, and police) than the support group members. These differences suggest that women who call the crisis line may be trying to define their experience (i.e., determine whether they are being abused) and explore their options (e.g., legal action, housing, counselors, etc.).

The Transtheoretical Model (Prochaska & DiClemente, 1982) suggests that individuals go through several stages during the process of changing an entrenched or addictive behavior. While women living in abusive relationships are not addicted to their abusers, the process they go through of recognizing and changing their abusive relationships is very similar to the stages posited by Prochaska and DiClemente. The Transtheoretical Model proposes that individuals go through five stages of change: precontemplation, contemplation, preparation, action, and maintenance.

Precontemplation is the stage at which there is no intention to change behavior in the foreseeable future (i.e., six months). Many individuals in this stage are unaware or not fully aware of their problems. Families, friends, or employers, however, are often well aware that these individuals have problems. "Precontemplators" may wish to change; but this seems to be quite different from intending to, or seriously considering, change in the near future. Resistance to recognizing or modifying a problem is the hallmark of this stage.

Contemplation is the stage in which people are aware that a problem exists and are seriously thinking about overcoming it, but have not yet made a commitment to take action. "Contemplators" may remain in this stage for long periods of time. Another important aspect of this stage is the weighing of the advantages and disadvantages of the problem and the solution to the problem.

Preparation is a stage that combines intention and behavior. Individuals in this stage are intending to take action in the next month and may have unsuccessfully taken action in the past year. People in this stage often have made attempts to change without reaching their goal. However, they intend to take action to reach their goal in the immediate future.

Action is the stage in which individuals modify their behavior, experiences, or environment in order to overcome their problems. Action involves the most overt behavioral changes and requires considerable commitment of time and energy. Individuals are classified in the action stage if they have successfully reached their goal for one day to six months. A significant, overt effort, and measurable change are the key elements of the action stage.

Maintenance is the stage in which people work to prevent relapse and consolidate the gains attained during the action stage. Maintenance is the continuation of change, not a static state, and may last a lifetime. The goal of maintenance is to stabilize the behavior change and avoid relapse or return to the unwanted behavior/situation.

While once thought of as a linear process, change actually takes a more cyclical course. Most people do not successfully maintain their goals on their first attempt. In fact, individuals may cycle through various stages many times before making the desired changes (Prochaska, DiClemente, & Norcross, 1992).

The data collected in this study suggest that crisis line callers may be in the contemplation or preparation stages of changing their abusive relationships. "Contemplators" may be attempting to determine the extent of their problem by talking about their situation with the volunteer phone counselors. Calling the crisis line also may be a way of gathering information about the pros and cons of staying in the relationship or trying to leave. The information collected in this manner may provide the incentive that the woman needs to plan for action. Women in the preparation stage may call the crisis line to find out about local resources that they may use once they take action. The large percentage of information and referral calls may indicate that many crisis line callers are in this stage.

Support group participants appear to be in one of three stages: preparation, action, or maintenance. A few women attend the group in order to learn more about domestic violence in order to help them decide what to do about their relationship. The majority of group members, however, seem to be taking action to leave their abusive relationships and/or to stay away from abusive partners once they have left. Over 80% of the support group participants were not living with their abusers, and were making other substantive changes in their lives to remain free of abuse (e.g., going to school, getting jobs, etc.). In addition, the cyclical pattern of change suggested by Prochaska and his colleagues (1992) can be seen in the repeated attempts that the support group subjects had made to leave their abusive relationships ($M = 3.5$).

Thus it appears that abused women may use different types of resources dependent upon where they are in their process of change. Women in the contemplation and preparation stages may be more likely to call an anonymous source for information regarding domestic violence and community resources. However, those women who are ready to make changes, or who need continued support for maintaining changes that they have already made, may be more likely to use a greater variety of services, particularly lawyers (presumably to aid in divorcing abusive spouses) and support groups (for mutual understanding and increased skills for living free of domestic abuse).

DEPRESSION, ANXIETY, AND SELF-ESTEEM

It is widely documented that depression, anxiety, and poor self-esteem are consequences of domestic violence (Douglas, 1986; Gelles & Straus, 1988; Koss, et al., 1995). Therefore, it was expected that participants reporting higher levels of overall severity of abuse would also report higher levels of depression and anxiety, and lower levels of self-esteem. However, the results of this study indicated that total amount of abuse did not provide predictive information on the level of depression and anxiety in this sample of abused women.

The levels of depression and anxiety extant in this sample are much higher than would be expected in a non-clinical sample. For example, Creamer and his colleagues (1995) used the BAI with a sample of 326 undergraduate students. They found that approximately 42% of their subjects were in the normal range, 35% were in the mild range, 17% were classified as moderately anxious, and only 6% were in the severe category. Perhaps the lack of variability in type and amount of abuse (i.e., the restricted range of abuse) resulted in limited ability to predict mental health consequences.

A complementary explanation for the lack of findings has a theoretical basis in the life events and depression literature. According to Brown and Harris (1978; 1989), depression can be "provoked by happenings in the environment" (1989, pg. 49). These environmental happenings, or life events, are stressors that occur during the course of living. Some of these life events are of a more moderate nature, and do not play an instrumental role in the development of depression. However, Brown and Harris posit that severe life events (e.g., loss of a job or a loved-one) combined with certain vulnerability factors (e.g., lack of intimate ties with a spouse) result in manifestation of depressive symptoms. Thus, once this critical mass of stress has been reached, the threshold of depression is crossed. Severe life events can, therefore, be seen as a dichotomous variable—absent or present.

Self-esteem and social support are two of the vulnerability factors identified by Brown and Harris (1989) as crucial in the development of depression. While determination of causal relationships is not possible in the study of women who have already been abused, it is clear that these women suffer from low self-esteem, and many have inadequate social support. For example, the participants in this study reported quite low levels of self-esteem, and rated family as not very helpful with abuse-related issues.

Viewed from within this model, the subjects in this study would all have experienced what Brown and Harris would undoubtedly characterize as severe life events (e.g., living in a life-threatening situation), coupled with low self-esteem and poor social support, and would all have crossed the depression threshold. Therefore, it would be difficult to detect any differences in their levels of depression based on the presence of severe life stressors in all of their lives.

It was hypothesized that depression, anxiety, and self-esteem would change as a function of whether or not a woman was still in her abusive relationship. The women's living status did not seem to predict their levels of depression or self-esteem; however, the small sample of women still living with their abusers appeared to have higher levels of anxiety. For those women who were no longer living with their abuser, length of separation was associated with levels of depression, but not anxiety or self-esteem.

In attempting to explain these inconsistent findings, a discussion of posttraumatic stress disorder (PTSD) is warranted. The diagnosis of PTSD has been created to describe the psychological sequelae of both chronic and one-time violence, perpetrated by an intimate or a stranger (Dutton, 1992; Kemp, et al., 1995). PTSD has been used as a framework for understanding clinical symptomatology resulting from a wide range of traumatic experiences that may be discrete (e.g., natural disaster, rape) or on-going (e.g., military combat, battering) (Davidson & Foa, 1993; Van der Kolk, 1987). Although the concept was initially constructed to explain reaction patterns in survivors of natural disasters and combatants in war, the PTSD construct has the advantage of providing a structure for examination of the effects of physical and psychological abuse on battered women.

The fourth edition of the Diagnostic and Statistical Manual of Mental Disorders (DSM-IV; American Psychiatric Association, 1994) characterizes PTSD as consisting of a set of responses to a traumatic event that must be of an "extreme (i.e., life-threatening) nature" (pg. 427). This "extreme" event is further defined as one that "involved actual or threatened death or serious injury, or a threat to the physical integrity of self or others" (pg. 427), and one in which the "person's response involved intense fear, helplessness, or horror" (pg. 428).

The DSM-IV identifies the hallmark symptoms of PTSD as 1) persistent re-experiencing of the event (e.g., intrusive thoughts, flashbacks, nightmares), 2) numbing of general responsiveness (e.g., detachment, inability to recall the event, lack of interest), and 3) increased arousal (e.g., sleeping disorders, irritability, difficulty concentrating). These symptoms must be present for more than one month, and must cause "clinically significant distress or impairment in ... functioning" (pg. 429). The onset of PTSD may be classified as delayed, if the symptoms do not appear until at least six month after the traumatic event.

Viewed within the PTSD framework, it is not surprising that level of abuse was not predictive of current levels of anxiety. If a single traumatic event can produce the symptoms associated with PTSD, then the repeated abuse experienced by participants in this study, while possibly exacerbating, would not be discriminative. In addition, the retrospective reporting of the abuse, the variability in onset of the symptoms, and the instrument used (i.e., the BAI) may have contributed to the lack of findings.

Interestingly, there was a strong positive correlation between several demographic variables and measures of anxiety (BAI), depression (BDI), and self-esteem (RSE). Income was the variable most highly correlated with anxiety, depression, and self-esteem. The lower the income, the higher the subjects scored on the BAI and BDI, and the lower they scored on the RSE. Adding this finding to the correlation between separation length and depression suggests that the problems associated with ending an abusive relationship and starting a new life (e.g., finding employment, housing, child care) may be more proximal to the survivor's mood than past abuse. The longer the subjects were separated from their abusers, the more they appeared to be adjusting to their independence.

This view is consistent with the life event literature. While service providers may regard leaving the abusive relationship as the best thing for a battered woman, the reality of going from a known situation to starting all over again, usually with children, no skills, and no place to live, may be a highly stressful event (or series of events). This type of stress, and the "social abuse" that occurs when one is unskilled, uneducated, and poor, may be a more salient risk factor for depression than even the most severe past abuse.

Given the above statistical and theoretical suppositions, it is understandable that the level of abuse experienced was not predictive of current levels of depression, anxiety, and self-esteem in the women who participated in this study.

RESEARCH/METHODOLOGICAL ISSUES

The results of this study have implications for research on the diagnosis, and treatment of victims of domestic violence. Specifically, this study addressed issues related to the assessment of services for abused women, assessment of domestic violence (particularly verbal and psychological abuse), and the consequences of those non-physical forms of abuse. The methodology used in this study provides a basis for the discussion of future research on domestic abuse.

The services reviewed and compared in this study are representative of those available to battered women throughout the state of Oregon, and many parts of the United States. Collaborative projects between domestic violence agencies, law enforcement, and criminal justice agencies have begun across the country. Such projects involve training police officers, district attorneys, and judges about the etiology and treatment of both survivors and perpetrators of domestic violence. In addition, many churches now offer financial assistance, day care, and counseling services to victims of family violence.   Little research has been done on the efficacy of these programs and services, and most of the program evaluation has been aimed at service levels goals (e.g., number and type of population served) rather than outcome variables (e.g., helpfulness). Yet these services and programs continue to operate in the same mode, and are often the only resources available to abused women. Assessment of these programs in a systematic manner needs to be done before conclusions can be drawn about their effectiveness.

With certain refinements, the measures used in this study could become the basis for a set of domestic violence assessments tools. The Support Group Survey was developed by interviewing domestic violence agency staff, volunteers, and former support group members. These women identified specific, measurable goals and objectives for the support groups. A small pilot study was conducted in which current support group participants also provided input into the identification of variables salient to the study of resource effectiveness. In addition, subjects in this study were given the opportunity, via open-ended questions, to provide detailed explanations of their responses and/or suggestions for improvement. The participants in this study were extremely receptive and appreciative of being included in both the design and data collection phases of the project.

This iterative process can be used by scientists and/or program evaluators to develop measures specific to their research. For each study of resource effectiveness, researchers should employ a process such as the one outlined above in order to carefully identify the relevant variables and outcome criteria. Then, measures should be developed to include both quantitative and qualitative questions, in order to allow the subjects to fully participate in, and inform, the research.

The result of this study indicating that verbal and psychological abuse are as harmful as physical and sexual abuse points to the need for improved assessment of non-physical forms of abuse. Community studies have yet to be done on non-physical abuse, primarily because of the difficulty in measurement. The standard assessment tool used in community, and most other, studies of abuse is the Conflict Tactics Scale (CTS) (Straus, 1979). The CTS is an 18-item scale which supposedly measures physical and psychological abuse. Frequencies are measured on a seven-point scale, ranging from "Never" to "More than 20 times per year." While the CTS is purported to contain 10 items that measure psychological abuse, on inspection, only five of the items are clearly related to psychological (or verbal) abuse (i.e., insulted you or swore at you; sulked or refused to talk about an issue; stomped out the room or house or yard; did or said something to spite you; threatened to hit or throw something at you). Four of the items are non-abusive conflict resolution skills (discussed an issue calmly; got information to back up his side of things; brought in or tried to bring in someone to help settle things; cried), and one is a physical abuse item (threw or smashed or hit or kicked something).

A variety of other measures have been developed during the last decade to assess for different types of abuse. The Inventory of Abuse (IA), used in this study, was adapted from the Wife Abuse Inventory (WAI) (Rodenburg and Fantuzzo, 1993). The WAI, a 64-item measure, was developed by the researchers in conjunction with abused women. The factor analysis of the measure clearly showed four types of abuse: physical, sexual, verbal, and psychological. While a 64-item scale is undeniably inappropriate (i.e., too time consuming and expensive) to be used in many studies, items with the highest loadings onto their corresponding factors could be used to develop a shorter, yet reliable measure of abuse.

The IA was adapted in this way, and was an accurate measure of the prevalence of the four types of abuse in this population. However, the open-ended format for reporting frequency of abuse presented interpretation problems for the incidence of abuse (i.e., a few participants responded with "hundreds of times" or "all the time" in the answer category requesting the number of times an event occurred in a six-month period). Future research might benefit from the development of a measure that combines a subset of the very detailed questions about abuse from the WAI and the seven-point frequency scale from the CTS.

In addition to the development of a comprehensive self-report measure, domestic violence assessment techniques must be developed for use in special settings (e.g., by therapists, physicians). Recent studies (O'Leary, Vivian, & Malone, 1992; McFarlane, Christoffel, Bateman, Miller, & Bullock, 1991) have shown that multi-modal techniques (e.g., questionnaire plus interview are significantly more accurate in detecting domestic violence than self-report surveys alone). More research in this area, comparing assessment strategies (e.g., self-report versus interview, versus a combination of both), may lead to a better understanding and method of assessment for domestic violence. Dissemination of successful assessment techniques may, in turn, enhance the way in which both researchers and clinicians identify all types of abuse.

This study did not find the expected relationship between abuse and depression, self-esteem, and anxiety. It is possible that given a larger sample, with more variability in history of abuse, or by using different measures, a relation between amount of abuse and depression, anxiety, and self-esteem could be established. Future studies might benefit from using interview measures, such as those developed by Brown & Harris (i.e., the Life Events and Difficulties Schedule, Self-Evaluation and Social Support Schedule) to study depression in battered women. Moreover, using measures of PTSD may yield more specific results than a general measure of anxiety such as that used in this study (i.e., the BAI). In addition, large-scale (i.e., community) studies of abuse and depression, anxiety, and self-esteem might also produce sample sizes with enough statistical power to detect the effects of abuse if they exist.

The subjects in this study reported more verbal abuse than physical, sexual, and psychological abuse combined, and more psychological abuse than either physical or sexual abuse. The frequency and perceived harmfulness of these non-physical types of abuse indicate that they may have severe consequences. Because the subjects in this study had experienced all types of abuse (and very frequent occurrence of abuse), it was impossible to identify specifically the effects of non-physical forms of abuse. Future studies should focus on the physical and mental health consequences of verbal and psychological abuse. By using measures such as those recommended above, researchers can examine the incidence and correlates of non-physical forms of abuse in a systematic manner.

Finally, an interesting line of research may be the application of the stages of change model to the study of battered women. Currently, the Transtheoretical Model is most often associated with the addiction literature. However, as outlined above, the model also describes well the process of change in survivors of domestic violence. While it may be somewhat dangerous to associate an addiction model with domestic violence (e.g., it may be taken out of context and used to further pathologize battered women), the application of the model may help to more accurately delineate the phases battered women go through in dealing with their abuse, and may lead to research on better (i.e., stage specific) treatment/program models.

TREATMENT IMPLICATIONS

The results of this study indicate that support groups and counselors are very useful to women seeking assistance with domestic violence. Specifically, providing support and encouragement, and information about abuse appear to be the most helpful factors associated with support groups and counselors. These findings have service implications for the providers/resources that were not as helpful to battered women (i.e., physicians, lawyers, police, clergy, and family).

Participants in this study suggested that all types of resources used (even support groups) needed to increase the amount of information they provide regarding domestic violence. For many of these resources, the first step in providing this information is self-education. Physicians, lawyers, clergy, family, and counselors, must learn more about domestic violence and it's consequences. They must also learn about all of the resources for battered women available in their community, and become familiar with the levels of service each provides.

It appears that physicians, lawyers, and clergy, need to improve their identification of domestic violence. These providers must ask specific questions of all of their clients regarding domestic violence, not just women whom they suspect are victims of abuse. In addition, it is important to directly ask specific questions regarding domestic violence, and not rely on the woman to self-identify her abuse. As stated above, multi-modal assessment is necessary in order to insure accurate identification of abuse. Using both written surveys and interview questions can help women to identify physical, sexual, verbal, and psychological abuse, all of which are perceived of as very harmful. By asking these questions, providers not only can identify targets for intervention, but they communicate their concern for the person's well-being, and convey that domestic violence is a real and serious problem.

In addition to identification of abuse, the results of this study suggest several areas of improvement for physicians. Battered women use physicians at a higher rate than do non-abused women (USDHHS, 1991; Browne, 1992); therefore, physicians have a unique opportunity to intervene with victims of domestic violence. Unfortunately, most physicians perceive barriers to dealing with domestic violence, one of which is the belief that they cannot be effective in helping battered women (Sugg & Inui, 1992). The results of this study clearly indicate that physicians can be effective in helping victims of domestic violence. Abused women rated physicians almost as highly as counselors and support groups. The findings from this study also suggest that physicians can improve their response to domestic violence by educating themselves and their patients about abuse, and the local resources (e.g., domestic violence agencies) available to survivors of domestic violence. Therefore, if physicians routinely assess for and discuss domestic violence with their patients, they can have an impact on the lives of battered women.

This study also points to a need for better understanding of the effects of non-physical forms of abuse. Physicians may treat women for depression and/or anxiety without assessing for verbal or psychological abuse. When symptoms are not taken in context, treatment (e.g., anti-depressant or anxiolytic medication) may be ineffective. Finally, physicians need to be aware of the symptoms associated with Post Traumatic Stress Disorder (PTSD) in order to recognize them in the diagnosis and treatment of battered women. As noted previously, more research, and communication of this research to clinicians, is needed to provide support for PTSD as a valid diagnostic category for abused women.

While rated as helpful in providing a safe place to discuss abuse, lawyers could benefit from continued education on legal ramifications of domestic violence (e.g., disadvantages of mediation in these cases). In addition, they might better serve their clients by being sensitive to the consequences of domestic violence (e.g., lowered self-esteem, depression, impaired decision-making). Battered women seeking legal advice may be unable to adequately assess their own legal and financial situation, and may need their attorney to be their advocate.

The police response to domestic violence has been changing over the last decade. Much conflicting research has been conducted on the effects of police intervention on domestic violence (Gelles, 1993; Jaffe, Wolfe, Telford, & Austin, 1986; Sherman, Schmidt, Rogan, Smith, Gartin, et al.; 1992). It is not the scope of this study to suggest changes to the criminal justice system response to domestic violence. However, the participants in this study indicated that the police needed to learn more about domestic violence, and to provide information and referrals to victims of abuse. Collaborative projects, such as discussed in Research/Methodological Issues section above, if successful, should be implemented on a large scale, in order to improve police response to battered women.

Utilization and helpfulness ratings of the clergy was quite low by participants in this study. How the clergy responds to the problem of domestic violence may in part be determined by theological beliefs, but it is also a product of the individual's knowledge, or lack of it, about the causes and consequences of domestic abuse. Studies have shown that the clergy are in denial about the prevalence of domestic violence in their congregation, or remain silent because of feelings of fear and defensiveness (Horton & Williamson, 1988). This silence must be broken by the clergy, whose position of leadership and responsibility gives them rare opportunities to educate their parishioners, and to help victims of domestic abuse. By re-evaluating traditional theology, and educating themselves about domestic violence, religious leaders can more effectively counsel abused women, and promote new, more egalitarian models of the family. Members of the clergy may also in the position to spend more time with battered women than many other types of service providers. Therefore, if the quality of information and support provided by the clergy could be improved, the utilization of religious leaders by abused women might increase.

Some might argue that it is unreasonable to expect physicians, lawyers and police to spend large amounts of time providing support, encouragement, and information to abused women. However, procedures can be developed within the medical or legal practice, or criminal justice system, that better serve survivors of domestic violence. For example, a nurse, support staff member, layperson, or social worker educated about domestic violence and local services could be incorporated into the system as an internal consultant to which the physician, attorney, or police officer could refer. Models such as these suggested are currently being tested in managed care medical (Thomas Thompson, Research Scientist, Group Health Cooperative of Puget Sound, personal communication, 1996; Diana Shye, Research Scientist, Center for Health Research, personal communication, 1996), and criminal justice (Susan Hadley, Director, Minnesota Coalition Against Domestic Violence, personal communication, 1996) settings.

An unusual finding of this study was the low helpfulness rating of family members. The participants in this study reported that family members, the most often used resource, were the least helpful. Comments by support group participants suggested that family members did not provide the non-judgmental support and encouragement that they needed. In addition, family members lack knowledge about the nature and consequences of domestic abuse. Increased public awareness and education about domestic violence may help the family and friends of abused women to be more knowledgable and understanding. For example, most domestic violence agencies encourage family members and friends to call the crisis line for information and referrals. They also welcome women who accompany survivors to support groups. By informing relatives and friends about domestic violence, and the processes of change, formal service providers may increase the helpfulness of the abused woman's support system, and increase the likelihood of a successful transition out of her abusive relationship.

In addition, domestic violence agencies and counselors may benefit from the direct application of the stages of change model to battered women. Although this step may be intuitively taken by many experienced clinicians, a more explicit model would enhance efficient, integrative, and prescriptive treatment plans. In addition, the stages of change research suggests that most people attempting to change will recycle several times through the stages before achieving long-term maintenance. Accordingly, intervention programs and personnel expecting people to progress linearly through the stages are likely to gather disappointing and discouraging results. On-going assessment, and awareness of the cyclical patterns of change, may enhance both the provider's and client's experience.

The current study complements other on-going research (Fisher, 1996) which indicates that different types of interventions may be needed at different stages of a problem (e.g., with victims of heart attack). These studies suggest that more direct intervention may be needed when the victim is in a crisis stage (i.e., immediately following a heart attack or an abusive incident), and that non-directive support and encouragement are needed in later stages (i.e., lifestyle changes for the heart attack victim or woman who has left her abuser). The women who participated in this study reported that different components of the support group were helpful at different times. These women stated that information about abuse, and referrals to local resources were most helpful when making a decision to leave, or shortly after leaving, an abusive relationship, while support and encouragement, and sharing of experiences with other abused women, were important on an on-going basis. Therefore, in order to supply the most appropriate level of service or support to survivors of domestic violence, providers should attempt to assess the survivor's stage within her process of change.

Finally, participants in this study reported that counselors, while already quite helpful, still need to continue to educate themselves about domestic violence. In addition, one of the most helpful items identified by the subjects was hearing from and talking to other abused women. No matter how skillful therapists are, they still cannot provide the type of empathy, support, and encouragement that is available within the context of a support group. Therefore, counselors and therapists would enhance service to their clients by providing them with referrals to community support groups and/or domestic violence agencies.

CONSTRAINTS/LIMITATIONS OF THE STUDY

The primary limitations of this study were the small sample size and the subject selection process. The small number of women in the support groups who used the clergy, and the smaller number of crisis line callers who attended a support group, prevented the ability to perform the most appropriate statistical procedure (i.e., MANOVA), or even to compare support group helpfulness to other resource ratings in the crisis line sample.

In addition, the crisis line sample was a very small proportion of total crisis line callers. While a large percentage of the crisis line caller who were asked to participate agreed, less than 10% of the crisis line callers were surveyed. This difficulty in collecting information about crisis line callers greatly limited not only the power to compare resource helpfulness, but also the generalizability of the findings.

Furthermore, the study was conducted in a geographically limited area. While attempts were made to collect data from 25 domestic violence agencies throughout the state of Oregon, only three agencies gathered data for this study. The demands on domestic violence agencies are great, and their resources are limited, making research a low priority for most. In addition, several domestic violence victim advocates and support group facilitators expressed concern over the assessment of their "clients." However, most of the domestic violence agencies that were contacted, expressed interest in this study, and expressed a willingness to participate in future studies if trained assessors/interviewers were provided to collect data.

An additional difficulty with this study occurred with the use of the Inventory of Abuse (IA). While the results clearly indicated that battered women perceived physical and non-physical abuse to be equally harmful, there was little variability in the harmfulness ratings. The IA currently consists of a four-point Likert-type harmfulness scale. If the scale had more points (e.g., six or seven), perhaps it would be able to discriminate between the upper levels of the harmfulness ratings with more precision. In addition, it would be informative to add a question to the scale which asks the subject to rank order the harmfulness of the physical, sexual, verbal, and psychological abuse experienced.

There are also enhancements that could be made to the resource helpfulness surveys. More qualitative research should be conducted to identify additional components of community, medical, and professional resources that are helpful to abused women. These items plus the current components should be included in crisis line surveys in order to compare component helpfulness ratings between crisis line callers and support group participants.

Another limitation of this study was the lack of follow-up to further explore the variables that influence program/service effectiveness. A methodological limitation to studying battered women is that follow-up cannot be conducted on a random basis. Due to safety issues and the need to avoid putting this population at risk of further abuse, follow-up can be conducted only with those participants who give prior consent. While no follow-up is planned at this time, future outcome studies will be greatly limited by this safety issue.

In summary, the small sample size, geographical location, and self-selected nature of the sample limit the generalizability of the findings. Future studies should target domestic violence agencies on a state-wide basis, and should provide trained telephone interviewers to perform telephone assessments in order to collect information on a larger, more representative sample of abused women. In addition, all research on abused women should weigh carefully the risks that assessment may pose on the subjects. Finally, improvements could be made to the measures, to increase the accuracy and value of the data.

Measures of Community and Professional Services

SUPPORT GROUP SURVEY

I. This section asks general questions about you.

1. Today's Date: _____

2. Your Birthdate: _____

3. Race/Ethnicity:
   ☐ Caucasian (white)
   ☐ African-American
   ☐ Asian, Pacific Islander
   ☐ Native American (American Indian)
   ☐ Other (please specify) _____
   Are you Hispanic/Latino?   ☐ Yes   ☐ No

4. Marital Status:
   ☐ Single
   ☐ Married
   ☐ Living with partner

5. Education Completed:
   ☐ Grades 0-8
   ☐ Grades 9-11

☐ High school graduate or equivalent
☐ Some college
☐ College graduate
☐ Post college

6. Employment status:
    ☐ Full time
    ☐ Part time
    ☐ Full time homemaker
    ☐ Student

7. If employed, what is your occupation or job? _____

8. If unemployed, would you like to be employed?
    ☐ Yes   ☐ No

9. If "Yes", do you think you have the skills to get a job right now?
    ☐ Yes   ☐ No

10. Estimated *household* annual income: $_____

11. Number of children: _____

12. Do your children live primarily with you?
    ☐ Yes   ☐ No

13. Do you have health insurance?
    ☐ Yes   ☐ No

14. Are you still living with your abusive partner?
    ☐ Yes   ☐ No

15. If "No" , how long have you been separated from your abusive
    partner? _____

16. How long have you been in (were you in) this abusive
    relationship? _____

17. Approximately how many times did you leave or make an attempt to leave this abusive relationship?
    ____ times

18. Approximately how many abusive partners have you had?
    ____ abusive partners

II. This section contains questions about your use of different types of community services.

Physicians

19. Do you have a primary care physician (family doctor)?
    ☐ Yes   ☐ No

20. If "Yes" to #19, have you visited your primary care physician (family doctor) in the last 6 months?
    ☐ Yes   ☐ No

21. If "Yes", did you go to the doctor because of abuse-related problems (either physical or emotional)?
    ☐ Yes ☐ No

22. If "Yes", overall, please rate how *helpful* the doctor was for meeting your needs: (Please circle your response.)

Not at All Helpful	Neither Helpful Nor Unhelpful	Somewhat Helpful	Very Helpful
1	2	3	4

23. Please rate your doctor's *helpfulness* in the following: (Please circle your response.)

    a. Providing a safe place to talk.

Not at All Helpful	Neither Helpful Nor Unhelpful	Somewhat Helpful	Very Helpful
1	2	3	4

b. Letting you know that you are not the only one in your
    situation.

Not at All Helpful	Neither Helpful Nor Unhelpful	Somewhat Helpful	Very Helpful
1	2	3	4

c. Providing information and referrals on domestic
    violence/abuse.

Not at All Helpful	Neither Helpful Nor Unhelpful	Somewhat Helpful	Very Helpful
1	2	3	4

d. Providing support and encouragement.

Not at All Helpful	Neither Helpful Nor Unhelpful	Somewhat Helpful	Very Helpful
1	2	3	4

24. If "No" to #19, why don't you have a primary care physician?
    (Please check all that apply)
    □ Just moved to the area
    □ Don't go to the doctor on a regular basis
    □ Can't afford to go to the doctor
    □ Don't have insurance
    □ Other (describe) _____

Lawyers

25. Have you ever contacted a lawyer regarding separation or divorce?
    □ Yes   □ No

26. If "Yes", overall, please rate how *helpful* the lawyer was for
    meeting your needs: (Please circle your response.)

Not at All Helpful	Neither Helpful Nor Unhelpful	Somewhat Helpful	Very Helpful
1	2	3	4

27. Please rate your lawyer's *helpfulness* in the following: (Please circle your response.)

    a. Providing a safe place to talk.

Not at All Helpful	Neither Helpful Nor Unhelpful	Somewhat Helpful	Very Helpful
1	2	3	4

    b. Letting you know that you are not the only one in your situation.

Not at All Helpful	Neither Helpful Nor Unhelpful	Somewhat Helpful	Very Helpful
1	2	3	4

    c. Providing information and referrals on domestic violence/abuse.

Not at All Helpful	Neither Helpful Nor Unhelpful	Somewhat Helpful	Very Helpful
1	2	3	4

    d. Providing support and encouragement.

Not at All Helpful	Neither Helpful Nor Unhelpful	Somewhat Helpful	Very Helpful
1	2	3	4

28. If "No" to #25, why haven't you contacted a lawyer? (Please check all that apply)
    ☐ Didn't have the need
    ☐ Don't believe in separation or divorce
    ☐ Can't afford a lawyer
    ☐ Don't qualify for Legal Aid
    ☐ Other (describe) _____

29. Have you ever filed a temporary restraining order against your abuser?
    ☐ Yes   ☐ No

30. If "Yes", did it protect you from your abuser?
    ☐ Yes   ☐ No

31. If "No", why haven't you filed a temporary restraining order?
    (Please check all that apply)
    ☐ Didn't have the need
    ☐ Afraid to go to court
    ☐ Don't know how to get one
    ☐ Don't think it would work
    ☐ Other (describe) _____

Police

32. Have you ever contacted the police regarding your abuse?
    ☐ Yes   ☐ No

33. If "Yes", did it protect you from your abuser?
    ☐ Yes   ☐ No

34. If "Yes" to #32, overall, please rate how *helpful* the police were
    for meeting your needs: (Please circle your response.)

Not at All Helpful	Neither Helpful Nor Unhelpful	Somewhat Helpful	Very Helpful
1	2	3	4

35. Please rate the police officers' *helpfulness* in the following:
    (Please circle your response.)

    a.   Providing a safe place to talk.

Not at All Helpful	Neither Helpful Nor Unhelpful	Somewhat Helpful	Very Helpful
1	2	3	4

    b.   Letting you know that you are not the only one in your
         situation.

Not at All Helpful	Neither Helpful Nor Unhelpful	Somewhat Helpful	Very Helpful
1	2	3	4

c. Providing information and referrals on domestic violence/abuse.

Not at All Helpful	Neither Helpful Nor Unhelpful	Somewhat Helpful	Very Helpful
1	2	3	4

d. Providing support and encouragement.

Not at All Helpful	Neither Helpful Nor Unhelpful	Somewhat Helpful	Very Helpful
1	2	3	4

36. If "No" to # 32, why haven't you contacted the police? (Please check all that apply)
    ☐ Didn't have the need
    ☐ Afraid it would make things worse
    ☐ Don't think they would help
    ☐ Afraid they would take away children
    ☐ Other (describe) _____

Clergy

37. Have you contacted a member of the clergy (priest, minister, rabbi) regarding your abuse?
    ☐ Yes   ☐ No

38. If "Yes", overall, please rate how **helpful** the clergy was for meeting your needs: (Please circle your response.)

Not at All Helpful	Neither Helpful Nor Unhelpful	Somewhat Helpful	Very Helpful
1	2	3	4

39. Please rate the clergy's **helpfulness** in the following: (Please circle your response.)

a. Providing a safe place to talk.

Not at All Helpful	Neither Helpful Nor Unhelpful	Somewhat Helpful	Very Helpful
1	2	3	4

b.   Letting you know that you are not the only one in your
     situation.

Not at All Helpful	Neither Helpful Nor Unhelpful	Somewhat Helpful	Very Helpful
1	2	3	4

c.   Providing information and referrals on domestic
     violence/abuse.

Not at All Helpful	Neither Helpful Nor Unhelpful	Somewhat Helpful	Very Helpful
1	2	3	4

d.   Providing support and encouragement.

Not at All Helpful	Neither Helpful Nor Unhelpful	Somewhat Helpful	Very Helpful
1	2	3	4

40. If "No" to #37, why haven't you contacted the clergy about your
     abuse? (Please check all that apply)

     ☐ Didn't have the need
     ☐ Afraid it would make things worse
     ☐ Don't think they would help
     ☐ Don't belong to a church or synagogue
     ☐ Other (describe) _____

Counselors/Therapists

41. Have you visited a counselor or therapist regarding your abuse?
         ☐ Yes   ☐ No

42. If "Yes", overall, please rate how ***helpful*** the counselor/therapist
     was for meeting your needs: (Please circle your response.)

Not at All Helpful	Neither Helpful Nor Unhelpful	Somewhat Helpful	Very Helpful
1	2	3	4

43. Please rate the couselor's/therapist's **helpfulness** in the following: (Please circle your response.)

    a. Providing a safe place to talk.

Not at All Helpful 1	Neither Helpful Nor Unhelpful 2	Somewhat Helpful 3	Very Helpful 4

    b. Letting you know that you are not the only one in your situation.

Not at All Helpful 1	Neither Helpful Nor Unhelpful 2	Somewhat Helpful 3	Very Helpful 4

    c. Providing information and referrals on domestic violence/abuse.

Not at All Helpful 1	Neither Helpful Nor Unhelpful 2	Somewhat Helpful 3	Very Helpful 4

    d. Providing support and encouragement.

Not at All Helpful 1	Neither Helpful Nor Unhelpful 2	Somewhat Helpful 3	Very Helpful 4

44 If "No" to #41, why haven't you contacted a counselor/therapist about your abuse? (Please check all that apply)

☐ Didn't have the need
☐ Can't afford counseling
☐ Don't think they would help
☐ Couldn't find low cost counseling
☐ Other (describe) _____

Family

45. Have you discussed the abuse with members of your family?

    ☐ Yes ☐ No

46. If "Yes", overall, please rate how *helpful* your family was for meeting your needs: (Please circle your response.)

Not at All Helpful	Neither Helpful Nor Unhelpful	Somewhat Helpful	Very Helpful
1	2	3	4

47. Please rate your family's *helpfulness* in the following: (Please circle your response.)

    a.   Providing a safe place to talk.

Not at All Helpful	Neither Helpful Nor Unhelpful	Somewhat Helpful	Very Helpful
1	2	3	4

    b.   Letting you know that you are not the only one in your situation.

Not at All Helpful	Neither Helpful Nor Unhelpful	Somewhat Helpful	Very Helpful
1	2	3	4

    c.   Providing information and referrals on domestic violence/abuse.

Not at All Helpful	Neither Helpful Nor Unhelpful	Somewhat Helpful	Very Helpful
1	2	3	4

    d.   Providing support and encouragement.

Not at All Helpful	Neither Helpful Nor Unhelpful	Somewhat Helpful	Very Helpful
1	2	3	4

48. If "No" to #45, why haven't you talked to your family about your abuse? (Please check all that apply)

    ☐ Didn't have the need
    ☐ Afraid it would make things worse
    ☐ Don't think they would help
    ☐ Am not allowed to talk to family
    ☐ Don't have family
    ☐ Other (describe) _____

III. **This section contains questions about this support group.**

49. How did you hear about this support group? (Check *all* that apply.)

    ☐ Crisis Line
    ☐ Shelter
    ☐ Friend
    ☐ Family member
    ☐ Counselor/Therapist
    ☐ Personal physician
    ☐ Emergency room physician _____
    ☐ Attorney/Judge
    ☐ Other (describe) _____

50. How long have you been attending this group?
    _____ days / weeks / months / years (Circle only one)

51. Approximately how many times have you attended this group?
    _____ times

52. Approximately how many times have you brought your children with you?   _____ times

53. Have you ever attended another support group at another location?
    ☐ Yes   ☐ No

54. Please rate the following reasons *you personally* may have for attending this support group: (Please circle your response.)

a. I wanted/needed a safe place to talk.

Not a Reason	A Slight Reason	A Moderate Reason	A Strong Reason
1	2	3	4

b. I wanted/needed to hear from other women in the same situation.

Not a Reason	A Slight Reason	A Moderate Reason	A Strong Reason
1	2	3	4

c. I wanted/needed information about domestic violence/abuse.

Not a Reason	A Slight Reason	A Moderate Reason	A Strong Reason
1	2	3	4

d. I wanted/needed support from other women.

Not a Reason	A Slight Reason	A Moderate Reason	A Strong Reason
1	2	3	4

e. I wanted/needed some time away from home for myself.

Not a Reason	A Slight Reason	A Moderate Reason	A Strong Reason
1	2	3	4

f. I wanted/needed to meet other women who might become friends.

Not a Reason	A Slight Reason	A Moderate Reason	A Strong Reason
1	2	3	4

g. I wanted/needed free child care and a break from being with
    my children.

Not a Reason	A Slight Reason	A Moderate Reason	A Strong Reason
1	2	3	4

h. I was told/ordered to attend the group by a judge.

Not a Reason	A Slight Reason	A Moderate Reason	A Strong Reason
1	2	3	4

i. I was told to attend the group by my counselor/therapist.

Not a Reason	A Slight Reason	A Moderate Reason	A Strong Reason
1	2	3	4

Do you have any other reasons for attending this group? (Please
describe) _____

_____
_____
_____

55. Overall, please rate how *helpful* the support group was for meeting
    your needs: (Please circle your response.)

Not at All Helpful	Neither Helpful Nor Unhelpful	Somewhat Helpful	Very Helpful
1	2	3	4

56. Please rate the *helpfulness* of the following parts of this group that
    you personally experienced: (Please circle your response.)
    a. Having a safe place to talk.

Did Not Experience	Not at All Helpful	Neither Helpful Nor Unhelpful	Somewhat Helpful	Very Helpful
0	1	2	3	4

b.   Hearing from other women in the same situation.

Did Not Experience	Not at All Helpful	Neither Helpful Nor Unhelpful	Somewhat Helpful	Very Helpful
0	1	2	3	4

c.   Receiving information about domestic violence/abuse.

Did Not Experience	Not at All Helpful	Neither Helpful Nor Unhelpful	Somewhat Helpful	Very Helpful
0	1	2	3	4

d.   Receiving support from other group members and/or facilitators.

Did Not Experience	Not at All Helpful	Neither Helpful Nor Unhelpful	Somewhat Helpful	Very Helpful
0	1	2	3	4

e.   Having some time away from home for myself.

Did Not Experience	Not at All Helpful	Neither Helpful Nor Unhelpful	Somewhat Helpful	Very Helpful
0	1	2	3	4

f.   Meeting other women who might become friends.

Did Not Experience	Not at All Helpful	Neither Helpful Nor Unhelpful	Somewhat Helpful	Very Helpful
0	1	2	3	4

g.   Receiving free child care and a break from being with my children.

Did Not Experience	Not at All Helpful	Neither Helpful Nor Unhelpful	Somewhat Helpful	Very Helpful
0	1	2	3	4

h.   Participating in facilitator-led discussions or group exercises.

Did Not Experience	Not at All Helpful	Neither Helpful Nor Unhelpful	Somewhat Helpful	Very Helpful
0	1	2	3	4

Did you find any other parts of this group helpful? (Please describe) _____

_____

_____

_____

_____

57. If you found any of the items in #56 to be "Somewhat Helpful" or "Very Helpful," please describe *why* you think those things help meet your needs? (Please write on back if necessary.)_____

_____

_____

_____

_____

58. If you found any of the items in #56 to be "Not at All Helpful," please describe *why* you think those things did NOT help meet your needs? (Please write on back if necessary.) _____

_____

_____

_____

_____

59. What would you like to see **added** to the support group to improve it? (Please write on back if necessary.) _____

_____

_____

_____

_____

60. What would you like to see **removed** from the support group to improve it? (Please write on back if necessary.) _____

_____

_____

_____

Comments (Please let us know if we've missed something you think is important): _____

_____

_____

_____

_____

Thank you for completing this survey!

CRISIS LINE SURVEY

1. What is your age: _____

2. Are you:
   - ☐ Caucasian (white)
   - ☐ African-American
   - ☐ Asian, Pacific Islander
   - ☐ Native American (American Indian)
   - ☐ Other (please specify) _____

   Are you Hispanic/Latino?   ☐ Yes   ☐ No

3. What is your Marital Status:
   - ☐ Single
   - ☐ Married
   - ☐ Living with partner

4. What level of education have you completed:
   - ☐ Grades 0-8
   - ☐ Grades 9-11
   - ☐ High school graduate or equivalent
   - ☐ Some college
   - ☐ College graduate
   - ☐ Post college

5. What is your current employment status:
   - ☐ Full time
   - ☐ Part time
   - ☐ Full time homemaker
   - ☐ Student

6. If employed, what is your occupation or job? _____

7. What is your estimated *household* annual income?: $ _____

8. Do you still have children living at home?
   ☐ Yes   ☐ No

9. Are you still living with your abusive partner?
   ☐ Yes   ☐ No

10. If you answered "No" to #8, how long have you been separated from your abusive partner? _____

11. How long have you been in (were you in) this abusive relationship? _____

12. Do you have health insurance?
    ☐ Yes   ☐ No

13. Do you have a primary care physician (family doctor)?
    ☐ Yes   ☐ No

14. If "Yes", have you visited your primary care physician (family doctor) in the last 6 months?
    ☐ Yes   ☐ No

15. If "Yes", did you go to the doctor because of abuse-related problems (either physical or emotional)?
    ☐ Yes   ☐ No

16. If "Yes", overall, please rate how *helpful* the doctor was for meeting your needs: (Please circle the response.)

Not at All Helpful	Neither Helpful Nor Unhelpful	Somewhat Helpful	Very Helpful
1	2	3	4

17. Have you ever contacted a lawyer regarding your abuse?
    ☐ Yes   ☐ No

18. If "Yes", overall, please rate how *helpful* the lawyer was for meeting your needs: (Please circle the response.)

Not at All Helpful	Neither Helpful Nor Unhelpful	Somewhat Helpful	Very Helpful
1	2	3	4

19. Have you ever contacted the police regarding your abuse?
    ☐ Yes   ☐ No

20. If "Yes", overall, please rate how *helpful* the police were for meeting your needs: (Please circle the response.)

Not at All Helpful	Neither Helpful Nor Unhelpful	Somewhat Helpful	Very Helpful
1	2	3	4

21. Have you ever contacted a member of the clergy (priest, minister, rabbi) about your abuse?
    ☐ Yes   ☐ No

22. If "Yes", overall, please rate how *helpful* the clergy was for meeting your needs: (Please circle the response.)

Not at All Helpful	Neither Helpful Nor Unhelpful	Somewhat Helpful	Very Helpful
1	2	3	4

23. Have you ever contacted a counselor/therapist regarding your abuse?
    ☐ Yes   ☐ No

24. If "Yes", overall, please rate how *helpful* the counselor/therapist was for meeting your needs: (Please circle the response.)

Not at All Helpful	Neither Helpful Nor Unhelpful	Somewhat Helpful	Very Helpful
1	2	3	4

25. Have you ever discussed y our abuse with family members?
    ☐ Yes   ☐ No

26. If "Yes", overall, please rate how ***helpful*** your family was for meeting your needs: (Please circle the response.)

Not at All Helpful	Neither Helpful Nor Unhelpful	Somewhat Helpful	Very Helpful
1	2	3	4

27. Have you ever attended one of the Womenspace support groups?
    ☐ Yes   ☐ No

28. If "Yes", overall, please rate how ***helpful*** the support group was for meeting your needs?

Not at All Helpful	Neither Helpful Nor Unhelpful	Somewhat Helpful	Very Helpful
1	2	3	4

Measures of Abuse

INVENTORY OF ABUSE

Please write in the number of times your partner did these actions to you during the *past six months*, or during the *last six months* of the time you and your partner were together. Also, please circle *one* answer for how hurt or upset you were by each action. If your partner did not do these actions, please write a zero (0) in the blank space.

Number of time this happened in past/last six months:

1. Your partner imprisoned you in your house _____

    How much did this hurt or upset you? (Please circle your response)

    | This Never Hurt or Upset Me | This Rarely Hurt or Upset Me | This Sometimes Hurt or Upset Me | This Often Hurt or Upset Me |

2. Your partner threw objects at you _____

    How much did this hurt or upset you? (Please circle your response)

    | This Never Hurt or Upset Me | This Rarely Hurt or Upset Me | This Sometimes Hurt or Upset Me | This Often Hurt or Upset Me |

3. Your partner called you a whore _____

   How much did this hurt or upset you? (Please circle your response)

   | This Never Hurt or Upset Me | This Rarely Hurt or Upset Me | This Sometimes Hurt or Upset Me | This Often Hurt or Upset Me |

4. Your partner squeezed your breasts _____

   How much did this hurt or upset you? (Please circle your response)

   | This Never Hurt or Upset Me | This Rarely Hurt or Upset Me | This Sometimes Hurt or Upset Me | This Often Hurt or Upset Me |

5. Your partner told you that you were crazy _____

   How much did this hurt or upset you? (Please circle your response)

   | This Never Hurt or Upset Me | This Rarely Hurt or Upset Me | This Sometimes Hurt or Upset Me | This Often Hurt or Upset Me |

6. Your partner put foreign objects in your vagina _____

   How much did this hurt or upset you? (Please circle your response)

   | This Never Hurt or Upset Me | This Rarely Hurt or Upset Me | This Sometimes Hurt or Upset Me | This Often Hurt or Upset Me |

7. Your partner bit you _____

   How much did this hurt or upset you? (Please circle your response)

   | This Never Hurt or Upset Me | This Rarely Hurt or Upset Me | This Sometimes Hurt or Upset Me | This Often Hurt or Upset Me |

8. Your partner held you down and cut your pubic hair _____

   How much did this hurt or upset you? (Please circle your response)

   | This Never Hurt or Upset Me | This Rarely Hurt or Upset Me | This Sometimes Hurt or Upset Me | This Often Hurt or Upset Me |

9. Your partner harassed you at work _____

    How much did this hurt or upset you? (Please circle your response)

    | This Never Hurt or Upset Me | This Rarely Hurt or Upset Me | This Sometimes Hurt or Upset Me | This Often Hurt or Upset Me |

10. Your partner locked you in the bedroom _____

    How much did this hurt or upset you? (Please circle your response)

    | This Never Hurt or Upset Me | This Rarely Hurt or Upset Me | This Sometimes Hurt or Upset Me | This Often Hurt or Upset Me |

11. Your partner tried to rape you _____

    How much did this hurt or upset you? (Please circle your response)

    | This Never Hurt or Upset Me | This Rarely Hurt or Upset Me | This Sometimes Hurt or Upset Me | This Often Hurt or Upset Me |

12. Your partner took your wallet leaving you stranded _____

    How much did this hurt or upset you? (Please circle your response)

    | This Never Hurt or Upset Me | This Rarely Hurt or Upset Me | This Sometimes Hurt or Upset Me | This Often Hurt or Upset Me |

13. Your partner punched you _____

    How much did this hurt or upset you? (Please circle your response)

    | This Never Hurt or Upset Me | This Rarely Hurt or Upset Me | This Sometimes Hurt or Upset Me | This Often Hurt or Upset Me |

14. Your partner stole your possessions _____

    How much did this hurt or upset you? (Please circle your response)

    | This Never Hurt or Upset Me | This Rarely Hurt or Upset Me | This Sometimes Hurt or Upset Me | This Often Hurt or Upset Me |

15 Your partner kicked you _____

How much did this hurt or upset you? (Please circle your response)

| This Never Hurt or Upset Me | This Rarely Hurt or Upset Me | This Sometimes Hurt or Upset Me | This Often Hurt or Upset Me |

16. Your partner took you car key _____

How much did this hurt or upset you? (Please circle your response)

| This Never Hurt or Upset Me | This Rarely Hurt or Upset Me | This Sometimes Hurt or Upset Me | This Often Hurt or Upset Me |

17. Your partner told you that no one would ever want you _____

How much did this hurt or upset you? (Please circle your response)

| This Never Hurt or Upset Me | This Rarely Hurt or Upset Me | This Sometimes Hurt or Upset Me | This Often Hurt or Upset Me |

18. Your partner disabled your car _____

How much did this hurt or upset you? (Please circle your response)

| This Never Hurt or Upset Me | This Rarely Hurt or Upset Me | This Sometimes Hurt or Upset Me | This Often Hurt or Upset Me |

19. Your partner told you that you were lazy _____

How much did this hurt or upset you? (Please circle your response)

| This Never Hurt or Upset Me | This Rarely Hurt or Upset Me | This Sometimes Hurt or Upset Me | This Often Hurt or Upset Me |

20. Your partner called you a bitch _____

How much did this hurt or upset you? (Please circle your response)

| This Never Hurt or Upset Me | This Rarely Hurt or Upset Me | This Sometimes Hurt or Upset Me | This Often Hurt or Upset Me |

21. Your partner hit you with a belt _____

    How much did this hurt or upset you? (Please circle your response)

    | This Never Hurt or Upset Me | This Rarely Hurt or Upset Me | This Sometimes Hurt or Upset Me | This Often Hurt or Upset Me |

22. Your partner raped you _____

    How much did this hurt or upset you? (Please circle your response)

    | This Never Hurt or Upset Me | This Rarely Hurt or Upset Me | This Sometimes Hurt or Upset Me | This Often Hurt or Upset Me |

23. Your partner threw you onto the furniture _____

    How much did this hurt or upset you? (Please circle your response)

    | This Never Hurt or Upset Me | This Rarely Hurt or Upset Me | This Sometimes Hurt or Upset Me | This Often Hurt or Upset Me |

24. Your partner harassed you over the telephone _____

    How much did this hurt or upset you? (Please circle your response)

    | This Never Hurt or Upset Me | This Rarely Hurt or Upset Me | This Sometimes Hurt or Upset Me | This Often Hurt or Upset Me |

25. Your partner told you that you were a horrible wife/partner

    _____

    How much did this hurt or upset you? (Please circle your response)

    | This Never Hurt or Upset Me | This Rarely Hurt or Upset Me | This Sometimes Hurt or Upset Me | This Often Hurt or Upset Me |

26. Your partner prostituted you _____

    How much did this hurt or upset you? (Please circle your response)

    | This Never Hurt or Upset Me | This Rarely Hurt or Upset Me | This Sometimes Hurt or Upset Me | This Often Hurt or Upset Me |

27. Your partner told you that you weren't good enough _____

How much did this hurt or upset you? (Please circle your response)

This Never Hurt or Upset Me	This Rarely Hurt or Upset Me	This Sometimes Hurt or Upset Me	This Often Hurt or Upset Me

28. Your partner shook you _____

How much did this hurt or upset you? (Please circle your response)

This Never Hurt or Upset Me	This Rarely Hurt or Upset Me	This Sometimes Hurt or Upset Me	This Often Hurt or Upset Me

29. Your partner forced you to have sex with other partners _____

How much did this hurt or upset you? (Please circle your response)

This Never Hurt or Upset Me	This Rarely Hurt or Upset Me	This Sometimes Hurt or Upset Me	This Often Hurt or Upset Me

30. Your partner treated you as a sex object _____

How much did this hurt or upset you? (Please circle your response)

This Never Hurt or Upset Me	This Rarely Hurt or Upset Me	This Sometimes Hurt or Upset Me	This Often Hurt or Upset Me

31. Your partner pushed you _____

How much did this hurt or upset you? (Please circle your response)

This Never Hurt or Upset Me	This Rarely Hurt or Upset Me	This Sometimes Hurt or Upset Me	This Often Hurt or Upset Me

32. Your partner told you that you were stupid _____

How much did this hurt or upset you? (Please circle your response)

This Never Hurt or Upset Me	This Rarely Hurt or Upset Me	This Sometimes Hurt or Upset Me	This Often Hurt or Upset Me

33. Your partner forced you to do unwanted sex acts _____

   How much did this hurt or upset you? (Please circle your response)

This Never Hurt or Upset Me	This Rarely Hurt or Upset Me	This Sometimes Hurt or Upset Me	This Often Hurt or Upset Me

34. Your partner stole food or money from you _____

   How much did this hurt or upset you? (Please circle your response)

This Never Hurt or Upset Me	This Rarely Hurt or Upset Me	This Sometimes Hurt or Upset Me	This Often Hurt or Upset Me

35. Your partner told you that you were ugly _____

   How much did this hurt or upset you? (Please circle your response)

This Never Hurt or Upset Me	This Rarely Hurt or Upset Me	This Sometimes Hurt or Upset Me	This Often Hurt or Upset Me

36. Your partner whipped you _____

   How much did this hurt or upset you? (Please circle your response)

This Never Hurt or Upset Me	This Rarely Hurt or Upset Me	This Sometimes Hurt or Upset Me	This Often Hurt or Upset Me

Thank you for completing this survey!

References

Beck, A.T., Epstein, N., Brown, G., & Steer, R.A. (1988). An inventory for measuring clinical anxiety: Psychometric properties. *Journal of Consulting and Clinical Psychology, 56,* 893-897.

Beck, A.T. & Steer, R. A. (1990). *Beck Anxiety Inventory Manual.* San Antonio: Harcourt Brace Jovanovich, Inc.

Beck, A.T., Steer, R. A., & Garbin, M. G. (1988). Psychometric properties of the Beck Depression Inventory: Twenty-five years of evaluation. *Clinical Psychology Review, 8,* 77-100.

Beck, A.T., Ward, C.H., Mendelson, M., Mock, J., & Erbaugh, J. (1961). An inventory for measuring depression. *Archives of General Psychiatry, 4,* 561-571.

Berk, R. A., Newton, P. J. & Berk, S. F. (1986). What a difference a day makes: An empirical study of the impact of shelters for battered women. *Journal of Marriage and the Family, 48,* 481-490.

Blackman, J. (1989). *Intimate violence: A study of injustice.* New York: Columbia University Press.

Bowker, L. H. (1983). *Beating wife beating.* Lexington, MA: Heath.

Bowker, L. H. (1986). *Ending the violence: A guidebook based on the experience of 1,000 battered wives.* Holmes Beach, FL: Learning Publications.

Bowker, L. H. (1988). The effect of methodology on subjective estimates of the differential effectiveness of personal strategies and help sources used by battered women. In G. T. Hotaling, D. Finkelhor, J. T. Kirkpatrick, M. A. Straus (Eds.), *Coping with family violence: Research and policy perspectives* (pp. 80-92). California: Sage Publications, Inc.

Bowker, L. H. & Maurer, L. (1986). The effectiveness of counseling services utilized by battered women. *Women & Therapy, 5,* 65-82.

Breiner, S. J. (1992). Observations of the abuse of women and children. *Psychological Reports, 70,* 153-154.

Brown, G. W. & Harris, T. O. (Eds.). (1978). *Social origins of depression: A study of psychiatric disorder in women.* London: Tavistock.

Brown, G. W. & Harris, T. O. (Eds.). (1989). *Life events and illness.* New York: The Guilford Press.

Brown, S. L. (1991). Counseling victims of violence. Alexandria, VA: The American Association for Counseling and Development.

Browne, A. (1992). Violence against women: Relevance for medical practitioners. *Journal of the American Medical Association, 267,* 3184-3187.

Browne, A. (1993). Violence against women by male partners: Prevalence, outcomes, and policy implications. *American Psychologist, 48,* 1077-1087.

Cadsky, O. & Crawford, M. (1988). Establishing batterer typologies in a clinical sample of men who assault their female partners. *Canadian Journal of Community Mental Health, 7,* 119-127.

Carmody, D.C. & Williams, K.R. (1987). Wife assault and perceptions of sanctions. *Violence and Victims, 2,* 25-38.

Cantos, A., Neidig, P. N., & O'Leary, K. D. (1991) *Gender differences in injury rates in domestic violence.* Unpublished manuscript, State University of New York, Stony Brook, NY.

Cascardi, M., O'Leary, K. D., Lawrence, E. E., & Schlee, K. A. (1995). Characteristics of women physically abused by their spouses and who seek treatment regarding marital conflict. *Journal of Consulting and Clinical Psychology, 63,* 616-623.

Cazenave, N. A. & Straus, M. A. (1990). Race, class, network embeddedness, and family violence: A search for potent support systems. In M. A. Straus & R. J. Gelles (Eds.), *Physical violence in American families* (pp. 321-339). New Brunswick: Transaction Publishers.

Cimino, J. J. & Dutton, M. A. (1991). *Factors influencing the development of PTSD in battered women.* Paper presented at the 99th annual convention of the American Psychological Association, San Francisco.

Cooper-White, P. (1990). Peer vs. clinical counseling: Is there a place for both in the battered women's movement? *Response to the Victimization of Women and Children, 13,* 2-6.

Creamer, M., Foran, J. & Bell, R. (1995). The Beck Anxiety Inventory in a non-clinical sample. *Behavior Research Therapy, 33,* 477-485.

Cryer, L. & Beutler, L. (1980). Group therapy: An alternative treatment approach for rape victims. *Journal of Sex and Marital Therapy, 6*, 40-46.

Davidson, J. R. & Foa, E. B. (Eds.). (1993). *Post-traumatic stress disorder: DSM-IV and beyond*. Washington, DC: American Psychiatric Press.

Deschner, J. P. (1984). *The hitting habit: Anger control for battering couples*. New York: The Free Press.

Deschner, J. P., McNeil, J. S. & Moore, M. G. (1986). A treatment model for batterers. *Social Casework, 67*, 55-60.

DSM-IV. (1994). Washington, DC: American Psychiatric Association.

Dobash, R. E. & Dobash, R. P. (1987). Violence towards wives. In, J. Orford (Ed.), *Treating the disorder, treating the family* (pp. 169-193). Baltimore: Johns, Hopkins University Press.

Dobash, R. E. & Dobash, R. P. (1992). *Women, violence and social change*. London: Routledge.

Donato, K. M. & Bowker, L. H. (1984). Understanding the help seeking behavior of battered women: A comparison of traditional service agencies and women's groups. *International Journal of Women's Studies, 7*, 99-109.

Douglas, M. A. (1986). The battered woman syndrome. In O. J. Sonkin (Ed.), *Domestic violence on trial: Psychological and legal dimensions of family violence* (pp. 39-54).

Dutton, D. G. (1987). The criminal justice response to wife assault. *Law and Human Behavior, 11*, 189-206.

Dutton, M. A. (1992). Empowering and healing the battered woman. New York: Springer Publishing Co.

Edelson, J. L. (1984). Working with men who batter. *Social Work, 29*, 237-242.

Ewing, C. P. (1987). *Battered women who kill: Psychological self-defense as legal justification*. Lexington, MA: Lexington, Books.

Fagan, J. & Browne, A. (1994). Violence between spouses and intimates: Physical aggression between women and men in intimate relationships. In A. J. Reiss, Jr. & J. A. Roth (Eds.), *Understanding and preventing violence* (pp. 115-292). Washington, DC: National Academy Press.

Faulk, M. (1974). Men who assault their wives. *Medicine, Science, and the Law, July*, 180-183.

Finkelhor, D., & Yllo, K. (1985). *License to rape: Sexual abuse of wives*. New York: Holt, Rinehart & Winston.

Fisher, E.B. (1996). *Psychological aspects of social support in chronic disease and health promotion*. Colloquium conducted at Oregon Research Insitute, Eugene, Oregon.

Foa, E.B., Rothbaum, B. O., Riggs, D. S., & Murdock, T. B. (1991). Treatment of posttraumatic stress disorder in rape victims: A comparison between cognitive-behavioral procedures and counseling. *Journal of Consulting and Clinical Psychology, 59,* 715-723.

Follingstad, D. R., Brennan, A. F., Hause, E. E., Polek, D. S., & Rutledge, L. L. (1991). Factors moderating physical and psychological symptoms of battered women. *Journal of Family Violence, 6,* 81-95.

Frank, E., Anderson, B., Stewart, B. D., Dancu, C., Hughes, C., & West, D. (1988). Efficacy of cognitive behavior therapy and systematic desensitization in the treatment of rape trauma. *Behavior Therapy, 19,* 403-420.

Frieze, I. H., Knoble, J., Washburn, C., & Zomnir, G. (1980). *Characteristics of battered women and their marriages.* Final report of NIMH grant #RO1 MH 30913). Pittsburgh: University of Pittsburgh Press.

Frieze, I. H. & Browne, A. (1989). Violence in marriage. In L. Ohlin & M. Tonry (Eds.), Family violence. *Crime and justice: A review of research* (pp. 163-218)). Chicago: University of Chicago Press.

Gamache, D. J., Edleson, J. L., & Schock, M. D. (1988). Coordinated police, judicial, and social service response to woman battering: A multiple-baseline evaluation across three communities. In G. T. Hotaling, D. Finkelhor, J. T. Kirkpatrick, M. A. Straus (Eds.), *Coping with family violence: Research and policy perspectives* (pp. 193-209). California: Sage Publications, Inc.

Geller, J. A. (1982). conjoint therapy: Staff training and treatment of the abuser and abused. In M. Roy (Ed.), *The abusive partner: An analysis of domestic battering,* (pp. 198-215). New York: Van Nostrand Reinhold.

Geller, J. A. (1992). *Breaking destructive patterns: Multiple strategies for treating partner abuse.* New York: The Free Press.

Geller, J. A. & Walsh, J. C. (1978). A treatment model for the abused spouse. *Victimology: An International Journal, 2,* 627-632.

Gelles, R. J. (1987). *Family Violence.* California: Sage Publications, Inc.

Gelles, R. J. (1993). Constrains against family violence: How well do they work? *American Behavioral Scientist, 36,* 575-586.

Gelles, R. J. & Cornell, C. P. (1990). *Intimate Violence in Families.* Newberry Park, CA: Sage Publications Inc.

Gelles, R. J. & Straus, M. A. (1988). *Intimate Violence: The definitive study of the causes and consequences of abuse in the American family.* New York: Simon and Schuster.

Gelles, R. J. & Straus, M. A. (1989). *Intimate Violence*. New York: Touchstone.

Gelles, R. J. & Straus, M. A. (1990). The medical and psychological costs of family violence. In M. A. Straus & R. J. Gelles (Eds.), *Physical violence in American families* (pp. 425-430). New Brunswick: Transaction Publishers.

Giles-Sims, J. (1983). *Wife battering: A systems theory approach*. New York: Guilford.

Gondolf, E. W. & Fisher, E. R. (1988). *Battered women as survivors: An alternative to treating learned helplessness.* Lexington, MA: Lexington Books.

Goodman, L. A., Koss, M. P., Russo, N. F. (1993). Violence against women: Mental health effects. Part I. Research findings. *Applied and Preventive Psychology, 2*, 79-89.

Gordon, J. S. (1996). [A Model for Assessing the Efficacy of Community Services for Abused Women]. Unpublished raw data.

Gordon, J. S. (in press). Community services for abused women: A review of perceived usefulness and efficacy. *Journal of Family Violence*.

Greenblatt, C. S. (1985). "Don't hit your wife . . . unless . . . ": Preliminary findings on normative support for the use of physical force by husbands. *International Journal of Victimology, 10*, 221-241.

Hamberger, L. K. & Hastings, J. E. (1991). Personality correlates of men who batter and nonviolent men: Some continuities and discontinuities. *Journal of Family Violence, 6*, 131-147.

Hamilton, B. & Coates, J. (1993). Perceived helpfulness and use of professional services by abused women. *Journal of Family Violence, 8*, 313-324.

Harris, J. (1986). Counseling violent couples using Walker's model. *Psychotherapy, 23*, 613-621.

Herman, J. (1992). *Trauma and Recovery*. New York: Basic Books.

Hershorn, M. & Rosenbaum, A. (1991). Over- vs. undercontrolled hostility: Application of the construct to the classification of maritally violent men. *Violence and Victims, 6*, 151-158.

Hilberman, E. (1980). Overview: The "wife-beater's wife" reconsidered. *American Journal of Psychiatry, 137*, 1336-1347.

Holtzworth-Munroe, A. & Stuart, G. L. (1994). Treatment of marital violence. In L. V. Creek, S. Knapp & T. L. Jackson (Eds.), *Innovations in clinical practice: A source book* (pp. 5-19). Sarasota, FL: Professional Resource Press.

Horton, A. L., Wilkins, M. M., & Wright, W. (1988). Women who ended abuse: What religious leaders and religion did for these victims. In A. L. Horton & J. A. Williamson (Eds.), *Abuse and Religion* (pp. 235-245). Lexington, MA: Lexington Books.

Hotaling, G.T. & Sugarman, D. B. (1986). An analysis of risk markers in husband to wife violence: The current state of knowledge. *Violence and Victims, 1*, 101- 124.

Hotaling, G.T. & Sugarman, D. B. (1990). A risk marker analysis of assaulted wives. *Journal of Family Violence, 5*, 1- 13.

Hurlbert, D. F., Whittaker, K. E., & Munoz, C. J. (1991). Etiological characteristics of abusive husbands. *Military Medicine, 156*, 670-675.

Jaffe, P., Wolfe, D. A., Telford, A., & Austin, G. (1986). The impact of police charges in incidents of wife abuse. *Journal of Family Violence, 1*, 37-49.

Johnson, I. M., Crowley, J., & Sigler, R. T. (1992). Agency response to domestic violence: Services provided to battered women. In E. C. Viano (Ed.), *Intimate violence: Interdisciplinary perspectives* (pp. 191-202). Washington, DC: Hemisphere.

Johnson, N. (1985). Police, social work and medical responses to battered women. In Johnson, N. (Ed.), *Marital Violence* (pp. 109-123). Boston: Routledge and Kegan Paul.

Kantor, G. K. & Straus, M. A. (1990). Response of victims and the police to assaults on wives. In M. A. Straus & R. J. Gelles (Eds.), *Physical violence in American families* (pp. 473-488). New Brunswick: Transaction Publishers.

Kemp, A., Green, B.L., Hovanitz, C. & Rawlings, E. I. (1995). Incidence and correlates of posttraumatic stress disorder in battered women: Shelter and community samples. *Journal of Interpersonal Violence, 10*, 43-44.

Klein, P. A. (1992). Efficacy of conjoint group treatment in therapy for spouse abuse. *Dissertation Abstracts International, 53*, 565.

Leeder, E. (1994). *Treating abuse in families: A feminist and community approach.* New York: Springer.

Lewis, B. Y. (1987). Psychosocial factors related to wife abuse. *Journal of Family Violence, 2*, 1- 10.

Lie, G. & Gentlewarrier, S. (1991). Intimate violence in lesbian relationships: Discussion of survey findings and practice implications. *Journal of Social Service Research, 15*, 41-59.

Loring, M. T., Clark, S., & Frost, C. (1994). A model of therapy for emotionally abused women. *Psychology, A Journal of Human Behavior, 31*, 9-16.

Magill, J. & Werk, A. (1985). A treatment model for marital violence. *Social Worker*, *53*, 61-64.

Mancoske, R. J., Standifer, D., & Cauley, C. (1994). The effectiveness of brief counseling services for battered women. *Research on Social Work Practice*, *4*, 53-63.

Margolin, G. (1979). Conjoint marital therapy to enhance anger management and reduce spouse abuse. *American Journal of Family Therapy*, *7*, 13-23.

Margolin, G. (1988). Interpersonal and intrapersonal factors associated with marital violence. In G. T. Hotaling, D. Finkelhor, J. T. Kirkpatrick, & M. A. Straus (Eds.), *Family abuse and it consequences: New directions for research* (pp. 203-217). New bury Park, CA: Sage.

Margolin, G & Burman, B. (1993). Wife abuse versus marital violence: Different terminologies, explanations, and solutions. Special Issue: Marital conflict. *Clinical Psychology Review*, *13*, 59-73.

McEvoy, A., Brookings, J. B., & Brown, C. E. (1983). Responses to battered women: Problems and strategies. *Social Casework: The Journal of Contemporary Social Work, February*, 92-96.

McFarlane, J., Christoffel, K. Bateman, L., Miller, V., & Bullock, L. Assessing for abuse: Self-report versus nurse interview. *Public Helath Nursing, 8*, 245-250.

Mitchell, R. E., & Hodson, C. A. (1983). *Battered women: The relationship of stress, support, and coping to adjustment.* Paper presented at the meeting of the American Psychological Association, Washington, DC.

Moewe, M. C. (1992, April, 5). The hidden violence: For richer and for poorer. *Fort Worth Star-Telegram*, p. A 12.

Murphy, C. M., Meyer, S. L., & O'Leary, K. D. (1993). Family of origin violence and MCMI-II psychopathology among partner assaultive men. *Violence and Victims, 8*, 165-176.

Murty, K. S. & Roebuck, J. B. (1992). An analysis of crisis calls by battered women in the city of Atlanta. In E. C. Viano (Ed.), *Intimate violence: Interdisciplinary perspectives* (pp. 61-70). Washington, DC: Hemisphere Publishing Corporation.

Neidig, P. H. & Friedman, D. H. (1984). *Spouse abuse: A treatment program for couples.* Champaign, IL: Research Press Company.

O'Leary, K. D., Curley, A., Rosenbaum, A., & Clarke, C. (1985). Assertion training for abused wives: A potentially hazardous treatment. *Journal of Marital and Family Therapy, 11*, 319-322.

O'Leary, K. D., Malone, J., & Tyree, A. (1994). Physical aggression in early marriage: Prerelationship and relationship effects. *Journal of Consulting and Clinical Psychology, 62,* 594-602.

O'Leary, K. D., Vivian, D, & Malone, J. (1992). Assessment of physical aggression against women in marriage: The need for multimodal assessment. *Behavioral Assessment, 14,* 5-14.

Oppel, R. (1992, April 5). Seizing control through pain. *Fort Worth Star-Telegram,* p. A12.

Pagelow, M. D. (1981). *Women battering: Victims and their experiences.* Beverly Hills, CA: Sage.

Pagelow, M. D. (1988). Marital Rape. In V. B. Van Hasselt, R. L. Morrison, A. S. Bellack, & M. Hersen (Eds.), *Handbook of family violence* (pp. 207-232). New York: Plenum.

Pagelow, M. D. (1992). Adult victims of domestic violence: Battered women. *Journal of Interpersonal Violence, 7,* 87-120.

Ploch, D. R. & Hastings, D. W. (1995). Some church; Some don't. *Journal for the Scientific Study of Religion, 34,* 507-515.

Pressman, B., Cameron, G., & Rothery, M. (1989). *Intervening with assaulted women: Current theory, research, and practice.* Hillsdale, NJ: Erlbaum.

Pressman, B. & Rothery, M. (1989). Introduction: Implications of assault against women for professional helpers. In B. Pressman, G. Cameron, & M. Rothery (Eds.), *Intervening with assaulted women: Current theory, research, and practice* (pp. 1-8). Hillsdale, JH: Erlbaum.

Prochaska, J. O. & DiClemente, C. C. (1982). Transtheoretical therapy: Toward a more integrative model of change. *Psychotherapy: Theory, Research and Practice, 19,* 275-288.

Prochaska, J. O. , DiClemente, C. C., & Norcross, J.C. (1992). In search of how people change: Applications to addictive behaviors. *American Psychologist, 47,* 1102-1114.

Randall, T. (1990). Domestic violence begets other problems of which physicians must be aware to be effective. *Journal of the American Medical Association, 264,* 940-943.

Resick, P. A., Jordan, C. G., Girelli, S. A., Hutter, C. K., & Dvorak, S. M. (1988). A comparative outcome study of behavioral group therapy for sexual assault victims. *Behavior Therapy, 19,* 385-401.

Rose, K. & Goss, J. *Domestic Violence Statistics.* National Criminal Justice Reference Service, Bureau of Justice Statistics, p. 12.

Rosenbaum, A. & O'Leary, K. D. (1981). Marital violence: Characteristics of abusive couples. *Journal of Consulting and Clinical Psychology, 49,* 63-71.

Rosenberg, M. (1965). *Society and the adolescent self-image.* Princeton, NJ: Princeton University Press.

Russell, D. E. H. (1982). *Rape in marriage.* New York: Macmillan.

Saunders, D. G. (1994). Posttraumatic stress symptom profiles of battered women: A comparison of survivors in two settings. *Violence and Victims, 9,* 31-44.

Schulman, M. (1979). *A survey of spousal violence against women in Kentucky.* Washington DC: Government Printing Office.

Sedlak, A. J. (1988). The use and psychosocial impact of a battered women's shelter. In G. T. Hotaling, D. Finkelhor, J. T. Kirkpatrick, M. A. Straus (Eds.), *Coping with family violence: Research and policy perspectives* (pp. 122-128). California: Sage Publications, Inc.

Seligman, M. P. (1975). *Helplessness: On depression, development and death.* San Francisco: Freeman.

Sherman, L. W., Schmidt, J. D., Rogan, D. P., Smith, D. A., Gartin, P. R., Cohn, E. G., Collins, D. J., Bacich, A. R. (1992). The variable effects of arrest on criminal careers: The Milwaukee domestic violence experiement. *Journal of Criminal Law and Criminology, 83,* 137-161.

Shields, N. M., MdCall, G. J., & Hanneke, C. R. (1988). Patterns of family and nonfamily violence: Violent husbands and violent men. *Violence and Victims, 3,* 83-97.

Shotland, L. & Straw, M. (1976). Bystander response to an assault: When a man attacks a woman. *Journal of Personality and Social Psychology, 34,* 990-999.

Sirles, E. A., Lipchik, E., & Kowalski, K. (1993). A consumer's perspective on domestic violence interventions. *Journal of Family Violence, 8,* 267-276.

Snyder, D. K. & Fruchtman, L. A. (1981). Differential patterns of wife abuse: A data-based typology. *Journal of Consulting and Clinical Psychology, 49,* 878-885.

Stahly, G. B. (1978). A review of select literature of spousal violence. *Victimology, 2,* 591-607.

Stark, E. (1980). Psychiatric perspectives on the abuse of women: A critical approach. In A. Lurie & E. Quitkin (Eds.), *Identification and treatment of spouse abuse.* New York: Conference Proceedings.

Stark, E., & Flitcraft, A. (1988). Violence among intimates: An epidemiological review. In V.B. Van Hasselt, R.L. Morrison, A.S.

Bellack, & M. Hersen (eds.), *Handbook of family violence* (pp. 293-318). New York: Plenum Press.

Stark, E., Flitcraft, A., & Frazier, W. (1979). Medicine and patriarchal violence: The social construction of a "private" event. *International Journal of Health Services, 9*, 461-493.

Stark, R. & McEvoy, J. (1970). Middle-class violence. *Psychology Today, 4*, 107-112.

Stets, J. E. & Straus, M. A. (1990). Gender differences in reporting marital violence and its medical and psychological consequences. In M. A. Straus & R. J. Gelles (Eds.), *Physical violence in American families* (pp. 151-165). New Brunswick: Transaction Publishers.

Straus, M. A. (1976). Sexual inequality, cultural norms and wife beating. *Victimology, 1*, 54-76.

Straus, M. A. (1980). Victims and aggressors in marital violence. *American Behavioral Scientist, 23*, 681-704.

Straus, M. A. (1990). The national family violence surveys. In M. A. Straus & R. J. Gelles (Eds.), *Physical violence in American families* (pp. 3-116). New Brunswick: Transaction Publishers.

Straus, M. A. & Gelles, R. J. (1990). How violent are American families? Estimates from the national family violence resurvey and other studies. In M. A. Straus & R. J. Gelles (Eds.), *Physical violence in American families* (pp. 95-112). New Brunswick: Transaction Publishers.

Sugg, N. K. & Inui, T. Primary care physicians' response to domestic violence: Opening Pandora's box. *Journal of the American Medical Association, 267*, 3157-3160.

Tolman, R. M. & Bennett, L. W. (1990). A review of quantitative research on men who batter. *Journal of Interpersonal Violence, 5*, 87-118.

Trimpey, M. L. (1989). Self-esteem and anxiety: Key issues in an abused women's support group. *Issues in Mental Health Nursing, 10*, 297-308.

Turner, S. & Frank, E. (1981). Behavior therapy in the treatment of rape victims. In L. Michelson, M. Hersen, & S. Turner (Eds.), *Future perspectives in behavior therapy*. New York: Plenum Press.

Tutty, L. M., Bidgood, B. A., & Rothery, M. A. (1993). Support groups for battered women: Research on their efficacy. *Journal of Family Violence, 8*, 325-343.

United States Department of Health and Human Services (1991). *Report of the Surgeon General of the United States.*

United States Department of Justice (1980). *Intimate victims: A study of violence among friends and relatives*. Washington, DC: US Government Printing Office.

Van der Kolk, B. A. (1987). *Psychological trauma*. Washington, DC: American Psychiatric Press.

Veronen, L. & Kilpatrick, D. (1983). Stress inoculation training as a treatment of rape victims' fears. In D. Meichenbaum & M. E. Jaremko (Eds.), *Stress reduction and prevention*. New York: Plenum Press.

Violence against women, A majority staff report, Committee on the Judiciary, United States Senate, 102nd Cong., 2d Sess. (1992).

Vivian, D. & Langhinrichsen-Rohling, J. (1994). Are bi-directionally violent couples mutually victimized? A gender-sensitive comparison. *Violence and Victims, 9,* 107-124.

Walker, L. (1979). *The battered woman*. New York: Harper and Row.

Walker, L. (1981). A feminist perspective on domestic violence. In R. B. Stuart (Ed.), *Violent Behavior: Social learning approaches to prediction, management and treatment* (pp. 102-115). New York: Brunner/Mazel.

Walker, L. (1984). *The battered woman syndrome*. New York: Springer.

Walker, L. (1991). Post-traumatic stress disorder in women: Diagnosis and treatment of battered women syndrome. *Psychotherapy, 28,* 21-29.

Walker, L. (1994). *Abused women and survivor therapy: A practical guide for the psychotherapist*. Washington, DC: American Psychological Association.

Woods, S.J. & Campbell, J. C. (1993). Posttraumatic stress in battered women: Does the diagnosis fit? *Issues in Mental Health Nursing, 14,* 173-186.

Yllo, K. (1984). The status of women, marital equality and violence against wives: A contextual analysis. *Journal of Family Issues, 5,* 307-320.

Yllo, K. (1988). Political and methodological debates in wife abuse research. In, K. Yllo and M. Bograd (Eds.), *Feminist perspectives on wife abuse* (pp. 28-50). Newbury Park, CA: Sage.

Index